Better Homes and Gardens®

celebrate the SEASON 2006

Meredith® Books
Des Moines, Iowa

Better Homes and Gardens®

Celebrate the Season. 2006

Editor: Vicki Christian
Food Editor: Jessica Saari
Contributing Editor: Jilann Severson
Contributing Food Editor: Winifred Moranville
Contributing Recipe Editor: Joyce Trollope
Contributing Art Director/Graphic Designer: Marisa Dirks
Copy Chief: Terri Fredrickson
Publishing Operations Manager: Karen Schirm
Senior Editor, Asset & Information Management: Phillip Morgan
Edit and Design Production Coordinator: Mary Lee Gavin
Editorial Assistants: Kaye Chabot, Cheryl Eckert
Book Production Managers: Pam Kvitne, Marjorie J. Schenkelberg,
Rick von Holdt, Mark Weaver
Contributing Copy Editor: Amy Spence
Contributing Proofreaders: Judy Friedman, Karen Grossman, Jody Speer
Contributing Indexer: Stephanie Reymann
Conributing Cover Photographer: Pete Krumhardt
Test Kitchen Director: Lynn Blanchard
Test Kitchen Product Supervisor: Maryellyn Krantz

Meredith Books

Executive Director, Editorial: Gregory H. Kayko
Executive Director, Design: Matt Strelecki
Managing Editor: Amy Tincher-Durik
Senior Editor/Group Manager: Jan Miller
Senior Associate Design Director: Ken Carlson

Publisher and Editor in Chief: James D. Blume
Editorial Director: Linda Raglan Cunningham
Executive Director, Marketing: Steve Malone
Executive Director, New Business Development: Todd M. Davis
Executive Director, Sales: Ken Zagor
Director, Operations: George A. Susral
Director, Production: Douglas M. Johnston
Director, Marketing: Amy Nichols
Business Director: Jim Leonard

Vice President and General Manager: Douglas J. Guendel

Better Homes and Gardens. Magazine

Executive Editor: John Riha
Creative Director: Bradford W.S. Hong
Managing Editor: Lamont D. Olson
Art Director: Michael D. Belknap
Senior Deputy Edior, Home Design: Oma Blaise Ford

Meredith Publishing Group

President: Jack Griffin
Executive Vice President: Bob Mate

Meredith Corporation

Chairman and Chief Executive Officer: William T. Kerr
President and Chief Operating Officer: Stephen M. Lacy

In Memoriam: E. T. Meredith III (1933—2003)

Our seal assures you that every recipe in *Better Homes and Gardens® Celebrate the Season 2006* has been tested in the Better Homes and Gardens Test Kitchen. This means that each recipe is practical and reliable, and meets our high standards of taste appeal. We guarantee your satisfaction with this book for as long as you own it.

All of us at Meredith® Books are dedicated to providing you with information and ideas to enhance your home. We welcome your comments and suggestions. Write to us at: Meredith Books Editorial Department, 1716 Locust St., Des Moines, IA 50309–3023.
Celebrate the Season is available by mail. To order editions from past years, call 800/627-5490.

"slow down, you move too fast."

Simon and Garfunkel crooned that line in their 1966 hit, *59th Street Bridge Song*. Forty years later, those words ring more truly than ever. No matter how many timesaving and electronic devices we have, it seems like we're still rushing from task to task and event to event. On the following pages, we'll show you ways to take it easy and enjoy the coming seasons.

A casual gathering on pages 78–87 guides you through a party based on sharing time and cooking experiences with friends. On pages 114–123, we feature a cookie and gift exchange that celebrates the joy of girlfriends. Throughout the book, quick and easy crafts and recipes mingle with those that require you to slow down and enjoy the creative process. Take pleasure in both the process and the end result, whether it's a make-it-tonight project or one that lets you while away the hours. This year, adapt the legendary duo's song a bit. Don't just "make the morning last." Make the whole season last.

Jilann Severson

Jilann Severson

holly and berry
evergreen wreath

■ Frame collectible ornaments with a narrow wreath. Use a purchased frame or build one from narrow wood strips. Clip 3-inch-long pieces of various evergreens and wire them together in bunches of three. Wire the bunches to the frame until it is covered. Add holly leaves and berries and artificial snowberries, wiring and gluing them in place. Wrap the wreath with loose loops of satin ribbon and hang the ornaments from the back of the wreath.

4

table *of* contents

setting the stage

Signal the season from fall through New Years with indoor and outdoor decorations, wreaths, ornaments, trees, and wrappings in colors and styles that offer up feelings of peace and joy.

gathering together

Welcome friends and family to your home with relaxing parties and luscious foods. Recipes and decorating ideas make entertaining fun for both the hosts and the guests.

5

giving from the heart

Handmade means heartfelt when it comes to holiday gifts. Create one-of-a-kind gifts for everyone on your list. A section on thrifty crafting makes it possible to give more gifts than ever before.

just for kids

Host a kids' crafting party and have as much fun as the guests. And don't forget that pets love gifts, too.

In a Twinkling

Easy decorations you can make in an evening's time.

Let the

SETTING the STAGE

good times roll. Bring a sense of celebration to your home with richly colored fall decorations, clever tablesettings, embellished ornaments, seasonal wreaths, vintage collectibles, charming angels, and novel gift wraps. They will make everyone want to stay and have some fun.

the perfect pear

One of fall's favorite fruits, the pear, takes center stage
as a decorating motif with its gentle colors and elegant shape.

Every autumn, produce stands overflow with gracefully shaped pears in a variety of sizes and colors. This year, take that same elegant shape to the table for designs rich in both color and motif. Appliqued place mats that double as a table runner and a topiary made of miniature artificial pears and gold leaves add fall touches. A decoupage tray and a centerpiece made of pears and rye bring pretty shapes to a dining room.

a pear tree

A traditional topiary shape takes on a whole new look when made with tiny pears and golden leaves. A birch bark trunk and aged pot fit with the casual feel of the pears while the gold leaves add contrast and interest with their elegance.

1 Rub gray and green paint onto the pot to give it an aged look. Let dry.

2 Center the branch in the pot and tack it in place with hot glue. Wedge pieces of florist's foam around the branch to hold it upright and straight. Glue the florist's foam and branch in place.

3 Press the other end of the branch into the plastic foam ball, centering it. If necessary, carve out a hole for the branch. Hot-glue the branch in place. Using tacky glue, affix a very light coating of moss over the ball. Glue additional moss over the florist's foam in the pot.

4 Spray-paint both sides of the leaves gold, letting the paint dry between coats. Trim the wire stems from the leaves.

5 Starting at the bottom, hot-glue a row of pears around the base of the ball. Work up the sides and to the top, gluing concentric rows of pears to the ball. Fit the pears together as tightly as possible. Always keep the bottom of the pear toward the ball but vary the angles slightly.

6 After completely covering the ball, glue leaves into the open spaces between the pears. See the photograph *above* for details.

- ☐ 10 full-size artificial pears
- ☐ awl or metal skewer
- ☐ toothpicks
- ☐ hot-glue gun and glue sticks
- ☐ 4 small bunches of rye
- ☐ florist's wire

row, row, row

Two rows of artificial pears glued and picked together form the simplest sort of centerpiece. Bundles of rye tucked into the spaces further the feeling of fall.

1 On a flat surface, position the pears in two equal rows of five pears, aligning the sides with each other and making sure they line up evenly. Measure up to the widest point of one pear and mark that point. Using an awl or skewer, make a very small hole to receive the toothpick. Repeat for all other pears.

Join two pears with a toothpick. Add a dot of hot glue to one pear, then slide the pears together. Repeat to form two rows of five pears. Repeat to join the rows. See the photograph directly *above* for details.

Divide the rye into small bundles. Wire the stems with florist's wire about one inch below the heads; trim away the excess stems. Slip a bundle into each open space between the rows of pears. See the photograph *above* for details.

NOTE: Other dried grasses or flowers may be used instead of rye. If desired, fresh flowers inserted into small water-filled florist's vials also can be used.

What You'll Need...

FOR SIX PLACE MATS:

☐ large paper for pattern

☐ cotton fabrics with a slight print in the following colors: 3 yards pale yellow for the front and 3 yards apple green for the back; 1 yard light yellow for the center; $1/4$ yard brown for the seeds; $1 1/2$ yards green print fabric for piping

☐ low-loft cotton quilt batting

☐ $1 1/2$ yards paper-backed fusible transfer web for joining appliqué fabrics

☐ $1/2$ yard $1/4$-inch-wide brown grosgrain ribbon for stems

☐ 12 yards narrow cording to cover

12

shapely setting

A simplified pear shape forms a place mat with appliqued seeds, a ribbon loop stem, and green piping to resemble the outer skin. The reversible place mat has a green print background that resembles an uncut pear.

1 Enlarge the pattern on *page 157* to scale and transfer it to paper. For each place mat, cut out a full front from pale yellow, a full back from apple green, and a piece from batting.

2 Fuse transfer web to the remaining fabrics. For each place mat, cut a center from light yellow and two brown seeds.

3 Following the manufacturer's directions, fuse the center and then the seeds to each place mat front. Using matching threads and a tight, narrow zigzag stitch, sew around the center and seeds. See the photograph directly *above* for details.

4 Cut bias strips from the remaining green fabric, piecing as necessary. Cover the cording to create piping. Beginning and ending at the top, pin or baste the piping to the fronts of the pears. Cut the ribbon into 3-inch lengths. Fold each piece in half to form a loop for the stem. Pin the stem to the top where the piping pieces join.

5 With right sides facing, sandwich together a front, batting, and back. Sew around the edges using a $1/4$-inch seam allowance. Leave an opening at the bottom for turning. Trim the seam allowances and clip the curves. Turn to the right side, press, and slip-stitch the opening closed.

6 For a table runner, lay the finished place mats at a slight angle and overlap them slightly. For interest, alternate front and back sides facing up. See the photograph *above* for details. To join the mats permanently, topstitch them together where the sections overlap. Hook-and-loop tape also can be used or the mats can be kept separate and simply placed one atop the other.

13

tray chic

Photocopies of pear botanical prints turn an unfinished wooden tray into an attractive serving or display piece. Look for copyright-free art books and clip art in bookstores, arts and crafts stores, and online.

1 Sand the tray smooth and wipe it with a tack cloth. Paint the tray apple green, sanding between coats. Rub yellow-green paint over the apple green. Let the paint dry completely.

2 Cut out the pear images and arrange them on the tray. See the photograph *right* for details. Arrange the images as desired, adding more if needed. Paint the backs with decoupage medium and glue them in place. Add three or more coats of decoupage medium over the top, letting it dry between coats and brushing in alternate directions for each coat.

3 After the tray dries, apply two or more coats of clear varnish.

14

fall colors

Capture the brilliant oranges, yellows, and greens of fall and brush them across easy outdoor decorations.

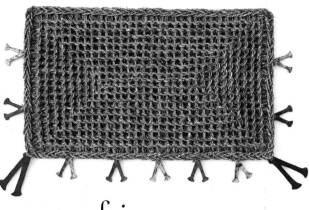

What You'll Need...

FOR THREE STANDS:

☐ two 42-inch-tall decorative pine newel posts

☐ saw

☐ fine sandpaper

☐ tack cloth

☐ outdoor acrylic paint in the following colors: apple green, dark green, orange, bright red, wine, bright yellow, and brown

☐ paper plate or other palette

☐ 1-inch-wide flat paintbrush

☐ three 4-inch-diameter round wooden plaques

☐ three 7-inch-diameter round wooden plaques

☐ drill and screwdriver

☐ wood glue

☐ 2-inch-long flathead screws

☐ three 2-inch-long nails

Take fall's bounty to new heights this year by elevating pumpkins and gourds on stands made from lumberyard newel posts. A sisal rug sports the same colors, bringing brilliance to even the gloomiest of days.

pumpkin stands

1 Saw off the tops of the newel posts to create flat tops. To make the two shorter stands, saw one newel post into two, cutting along a design line about 12 inches from the most shapely end. Sand all surfaces and wipe with a tack cloth.

2 Paint each section of the stands a different color using the design lines as natural color breaks. Lightly sand and paint again. Paint the large plaques to match the bottoms of the newel posts and the small circles to match the tops.

3 Squeeze brown paint onto a paper plate or other palette. Dip the bristle tips of the paintbrush into the paint, then wipe it almost dry on paper or the palette. Swipe the dry brush in diagonal X patterns over all the pieces. See the photograph *opposite* for details.

4 Center a large plaque on the bottom of each newel post. Glue and screw each plaque in place to form a base.

5 Drill a hole through the center of each small plaque. Drill two more holes, spacing each new hole ½ inch on either side of the center hole; the three holes should be in a straight line. Working from the back, drive a nail through each outer hole so the nails protrude through to the right side. These will form the prongs to hold the gourds in place.

6

Apply glue to the top of the newel post and screw it in place, taking care when working around the nails. See the photograph *above* for details.

7 The finished stands will have two nails sticking up from the top plaque to hold the gourds in place. See the photograph *right* for details. For safety, cover the nails when storing the stands.

v-fringe sisal rug

1 Sand all the letters and wipe them with a tack cloth. Paint them in the same manner as the Pumpkin Stands.

2 Drill a small hole through the bottom of each V. Thread the needle with the jute. Sew a large V to each front corner of the rug, knotting the jute on the back of the rug. Arrange the remaining Vs around the front and sides of the rug, spacing them evenly. Sew them to the rug in the same manner to form the remaining fringe. See the photograph *above top* for details.

What You'll Need...

☐ 2 large and 9 medium wooden V letters

☐ fine sandpaper

☐ tack cloth

☐ outdoor acrylic paint in the following colors: wine, brown, orange, dark green, apple green, bright red, and bright yellow

☐ paper plate or other palette

☐ 1-inch-wide flat paintbrush

☐ drill

☐ jute string or twine

☐ darning needle

☐ loose-weave sisal door mat

Thread the needle with jute. Arrange the Os in a circle. Use the jute to join the Os, wrapping each set five times. See the photograph above for details.

OOO, so clever

❧ Wooden Os tied to a twine-wrapped base form a rustic yet whimsical wreath. Brown paint dry-brushed over the letters keeps their colors from becoming too garish.

1 *Sand all the Os and wipe with a tack cloth. Paint the Os in the manner described for the Pumpkin Stands on page 15.*

2 *Wrap the wreath form with jute. See the photograph above right for details.*

Place the Os over the wrapped wreath form. Using the needle and twine, attach the Os to the wreath form with large cross-stitches. See the photograph above for details.

► Hanging Around
This autumnal version of a May Basket is perfect to hang on door handles or window locks. Choose a small jar or votive cup that has a lip or ridges at the top. Wrap wire around the jar several times, placing it between the ridges or under the lip. Twist the ends into a hanging loop. Fill the jar with water and a collection of fall herbs, pods, flowers, and berries.

In a Twinkling

fall into it

◄ Come On In Use fall's finest to create an easy welcome plaque for your door or entry table. Pick a warm-hued wooden frame and select coordinating decorative paper from the scrapbooking department. Print or hand-letter the word "Welcome" on the paper so it fits within the frame. Cut the paper to fit the frame. Using double-sided tape, adhere pressed leaves to the paper. Place the paper in the frame and reassemble the frame, omitting the glass.

◀ Making Scents Add a gentle fragrance to your rooms with potpourri balls. Use a single element such as dried orange peel or bay leaves, or mix it up with purchased potpourri. Attach the potpourri to 3-inch-diameter plastic foam balls using hot glue and sequin pins, making sure the foam and pins are covered.

▶ Decorating on a String
Tie little gourds, orange peels, leaves, and other natural elements into a short garland, bringing a touch of fall to a window, mirror, picture frame, doorway, or other small space. Here dried loofah gourds are the focal point, but any small gourd will work. To join the items, make a hole using a small punch for pieces like leaves and a drill for dried orange peel, then knot them onto string or twine. The gourds can be tied in place.

19

◀ Fall Nesting Give a crafts store bird's nest a fall look by filling it with painted acorns, seed pods, or other fall gatherings. To paint the acorns, brush or dip the lower half in acrylic paint. Place the nest on a plate to keep things tidy.

seasonal wreaths

Welcome guests into your home with wreaths that use natural elements to reflect the best of fall and winter.

the luck of fall

❧ A horseshoe-shape wreath packed with wheat gives a hint of luck and good harvest.

Cut the top portion from a round plastic foam wreath to form the horseshoe shape. Gather wheat into small bundles and wire the stems together. Using U-shape florist's pins and starting at the upper points of the horseshoe, pin the bundles to the wreath. Work your way down so each set of bundles covers the stems and wires of the previous bundle. Trim the stems short for the bottom bundles.

Hot-glue dried seed heads to the center of the wreath to hide the stems and wires.

lean and green

❧ Miniature gourds and gathered leaves are a slight departure from the traditional fall wreath when done all in various shades of green.

Gather small green gourds and green maple leaves or purchase silk versions at crafts stores. Using a long and fine bit, drill through the gourds. Offset the hole slightly toward the back of each gourd. Wire the gourds to a round straw wreath form.

Hot-glue green maple leaves between the spaces so all the straw is covered.

berry beautiful

◥ A wreath that is natural in elements and shape adds grace to your home when it's comprised of wispy greens and bright berries.

Purchase a narrow twig wreath in the desired size. One that is loosely wrapped and has small branches extending out works best. Hot-glue seeded eucalyptus and white pine to the wreath form, allowing some of the twigs to show through. Add red and white berries, working their stems between the branches of the wreath and securing them with hot glue as needed.

festive fruits

◥ Oranges add color and a sweet scent to a wreath that's packed with leaves, berries, and flowers.

Run a skewer through fresh or artificial oranges, keeping the holes slightly to the back half of the oranges. Work heavy florist's wire through the holes. Wire the oranges to a wide wooden picture frame. (An unfinished frame works best.) Fill in the spaces between the oranges by hot-gluing bittersweet, green yarrow, thistle-like orange safflowers, aspen or birch leaves, or any other combination of seasonal flowers, leaves, and berries.

Tack wide silk ribbon to the back of the frame at each upper corner. Hang the wreath by the frame, then draw the ribbons up into a bow so it appears the wreath hangs from the ribbons.

give them the brush

Miniature trees with their stiff bristle boughs and twisted wire trunks are one of the hot Christmas collectibles.

Glitzy, gaudy aluminum Christmas trees and their slowly turning color wheels made a comeback a few years ago, followed by a rush on vintage ornaments and tree toppers. Is it any surprise that another icon of the 1950s and 1960s—the bottlebrush tree—is becoming a trendy Christmas collectible? Although production goes back to the 1920s, it was three decades later that the trees took on a "modern" look and their popularity increased. In the 1950s, they began showing up in colors other than the standard green. They also started sporting snow, garlands, and miniature ornaments. Many a home—and even a few nativity sets—were adorned with these little trees as diminutive vignettes with plastic Santas, snowmen, and reindeer figures were set up on coffee tables and hutches. Today, a grove of trees may be a feature display and elevated to the foreground instead of being a backdrop for other items. Collectors often look for unusual colors, ornamentation, or a variety of sizes. As with any collectible, reproductions are now flooding the market. Bottlebrush trees can be found on the shelves of holiday stores as well as the cabinets of antiques shops.

25

A trio of ivory-colored trees flanks a cherubic garden statue while others stand in the background for a sophisticated still life. Ornaments such as foil reflectors or handmade decorations make trees highly collectible.

Tiny cardboard buildings and a cluster of trees that are heavily decorated with ornaments and plaster snow create a nostalgic display on a tray and sideboard. For more on the cardboard houses, see *page 38.*

Bottlebrush trees were introduced in the 1920s when it first became possible to make brushes by machine. Made from a twisted wire core embedded with bristles, the trees were assembled in the same way as utilitarian bottle-scrubbing brushes. When the brush was trimmed into a conical shape and had a disk added for a base, it became a tree. Hence the name bottlebrush tree. The technique worked for brushes from 1 to 14 inches tall, ensuring that the bottlebrush tree always would be associated with miniatures.

In the 1950s, the trees took on the colors of the era to match modern decor. Pink, blue, red, and yellow-green are some of the more common hues from that colorful age. Small decorations and strands of garlands also started showing up. Many of the trees sported clumps of snow, usually made from plaster.

Look for vintage trees at antiques shops and shows and at online auctions. Original prices were usually under a dollar. Today they sell for anywhere from a few dollars to around $50.

☙ Smaller trees are easier to find. The pink ones are likely from the 50s or 60s; prior to that, green was the favored color. Tiny trees take on a graphic look when lined up on a window ledge or mantel, but take care not to expose vintage trees to sunlight.

☙ Larger trees measure in at about a foot tall and are more likely to be adorned with ornaments, foil, and garlands. If the wooden disk base is damaged or missing, plant the tree in a container filled with florist's foam. Cover the florist's foam with artificial snow or glittered felt.

☙ Less common are trees with fruits or other ornaments. Often these were created by the original owner who glued items to a plain tree. Do the same with reproduction trees for a themed look. Adding items to a vintage tree can decrease its value.

winter garden

Honor the growing season with a tree that sprouts from a watering can. Urns, clay pots, birdhouses, wheelbarrows, and miniature gardening tools pack a tree topped with a finial.

Wrap the tree with lights. Fill a watering can with florist's foam. Remove any of the tree base that will not fit into the opening of the watering can. Center the tree in the watering can and secure it with more florist's foam. Hot-glue the tree trunk and florist's foam if necessary.

Using thin green florist's wire, attach clusters of artificial red berries to the tips of the tree branches.

Check gift shops, holiday departments, crafts stores, and gardening stores for miniatures to decorate the tree. For the gazing balls, hot-glue small ornaments into miniature urns. For the clay pots, hot-glue sprigs of artificial holly inside the pots and narrow red ribbon under the rim on the outside. Tie the ribbon ends in a knot and leave long tails.

Tie the pots to the tree. Use wire or ribbon to attach the remaining items to the tree. Slide a small finial over the top branch of the tree for the topper.

personality trees

A forest of tiny silk trees reflects the interests of each family member. They're so fun, you'll want one for each room.

christmas tea

A little tree steeped in the tradition of a Christmas tea party displays pieces from doll- and child-size tea sets. A white fairy joins the party on a tree that's topped with a holiday book and perched in an old teapot.

String the tree with lights. Pack an old or inexpensive teapot with florist's foam. Remove any of the base of the tree that will not fit into the teapot opening and center the tree in the teapot. Add more florist's foam to fill in any gaps. If needed, use hot glue to secure the foam and tree.

If a fairy or doll will be used, place it in the tree. Use ribbon, wire, or hot glue to secure it if necessary.

Hot-glue the components of the tea sets together. For example, glue lids to teapots and sugar bowls, cups to saucers, and flatware to plates. Use narrow green florist's wire to secure the china to the tree. Add ribbons to cover the wires if desired.

Top the tree with a teacup and saucer. If available, add a small Christmas book to the top. Check toy stores, miniatures departments, crafts stores, and holiday decorating sections for similar books as well as the tea sets.

29

sew festive

Have guests in stitches over a tree done up in sewing notions and placed in an old sewing basket. Both new and old buttons, scissors, thimbles, thread spools, pincushions, and measuring tapes adorn the petite tree.

String lights onto the tree. Place the tree into a sewing basket. If necessary, secure it with florist's clay or hot glue.

Use narrow green florist's wire or ribbon to attach the sewing notions to the tree. Spools of thread can be slipped over the branch tips. To hold thimbles to other branch tips, place a small ball of florist's clay inside the thimble before slipping the thimble onto the tip of the tree branch.

For the button ornaments, run thin black wire through two button holes or the button shank. Twist the wire on itself, leaving a long tail. Slide the wire tail between the branches.

Finish the tree with garlands of measuring tapes and narrow trims.

nursery times

Whether it's Old MacDonald's crew or the cow that jumped over the moon, animals go hoof-in-hand with nursery rhymes. In a young child's room, miniature animals perch on the branches of a tree that is planted in a toy barn base. For a topper, the proverbial cow jumps onto the moon.

Attach cluster lights to a small artificial tree, spacing them evenly. Tie small animals to the branches with twine or jute.

To make the EIEIO signs, stick the appropriate self-adhesive crafts foam letters onto brown crafts foam. Cut around the letters to form the sign and hang the sign with twine or jute.

For the top, cut a crescent shape from lightweight cardboard for the moon. Paint the moon off-white.

If desired, while the paint is wet, sprinkle it with glitter. Place the moon at the the tree top. If needed, wire it in place by taping wire to the back of the cardboard and wrapping it around tree branches. Perch a cow on the moon.

Place the finished tree in a vintage, reproduction, or new toy barn and run the light cord out a door or window in the back of the barn.

What You'll Need...

FOR THE HANGERS:

- [ ] 18-gauge black wire such as annealed mechanic's wire (available at crafts and hardware stores)
- [ ] wire cutters
- [ ] needle-nose pliers
- [ ] pencil
- [ ] heavy duty thread
- [ ] hot-glue gun and glue sticks

FOR THE ORNAMENTS:

- [ ] boiled wool or wool felt in the desired colors
- [ ] low-loft polyester or cotton quilt batting
- [ ] embroidery floss
- [ ] trims such as pom-poms and buttons (see the specific ornaments for details)

folk art favorites

Spread a feeling of warmth and nostalgia with ornaments and stockings inspired by traditional folk arts.

These felt trims are inspired by British, American, and Scandinavian folk crafts. To learn more of their history, see *page 36*.

pearly greats tree ornament

FOR THE 10-BUTTON TREE

Enlarge the patterns on *page 155* to scale. Cut out two black trees and a green inner appliqué. Sew the appliqué to the ornament front.

Sew rows of 7/16-inch buttons to the appliqué section. See the photograph *left* for details on button placement.

Cut the batting using the smaller tree shape. Baste the batting to the wrong side of the ornament back. Make a hanger according to the directions *right*. Hot-glue the ornament hook to the top of the tree so the thread-wrapped base will be encased. With wrong sides facing, whipstitch the ornament front to the ornament back.

FOR THE 3-BUTTON TREE

Make the ornament as described *above* using green for the trees and black for the appliqué. Instead of 10 buttons, sew three buttons vertically onto the appliqué. Starting at the bottom, sew on a 7/8-inch, a 3/4-inch, and a 7/16-inch button.

Assemble the ornament as described for the 10-button tree.

lucky pennies tree ornament

FOR THE SINGLE-PENNY TREE ORNAMENT

Enlarge the pattern on *page 155*. Cut four trees from gold. Cut four concentric circles from wool or felt scraps with the largest circle being 2 1/2 inches in diameter. Using a long stitch, sew the circles on top of each other and to the ornament front.

Assemble the ornament as described for the Pearly Greats Ornament *left*.

FOR THE THREE-PENNY TREE ORNAMENT

Enlarge the pattern on *page 155*. Cut four trees from gold. Cut three 1 3/8-inch-diameter circles and three 7/8-inch-diameter circles from the desired colors. Using long stitches, sew a smaller circle to each larger circle. Arrange the three circles on the ornament front and embroider them in place. See the photograph *left* for details.

Assemble the ornament as described for the Pearly Greats Ornament *left*.

nordic treasures tree ornament

FOR THE 15-POM-POM TREE

Enlarge the pattern on *page 155* to scale. Cut two complete trees from white and one trunk from red. Appliqué the trunk to the tree.

Hot-glue rows of small purchased pom-poms to the tree. See the photograph *left* for details.

Assemble the ornament as described for the Pearly Greats Ornament *left*.

FOR THE 11-POM-POM TREE

Cut two complete trees from red and one base and trunk from gold. Appliqué the base and trunk to the ornament front.

Hot-glue small purchased pom-poms to the trunk and bottom of the tree. See the photograph *left* for details.

Assemble the ornament as described for the Pearly Greats Ornament *left*.

TO MAKE A HANGER

Cut a 6 1/2-inch length of wire. Fold it in half to make a tight U-shape. Using the pliers, make a tight circle on each end.

Curl the ends back into a loose spiral. See the photograph *left* for details.

Cut an 8-inch length of wire. Wrap it around a pencil at the center and twist the wire tightly on itself. Continue twisting until the twisted strand is 2 1/2 inches long. Cut the wire so the twisted portion is 2 1/4 inches long.

Slip the twisted wire into the U-shape of the curled wire. Using heavy thread, wrap the base of the U to hold the pieces together. Secure the pieces with hot glue.

What You'll Need...

- [ ] ²/₃ yard boiled wool
- [ ] ½ yard black velvet
- [ ] various white buttons
- [ ] black thread
- [ ] 1 yard white satin cord for the hanger

What You'll Need...

- [ ] high-quality wool felt in the following amounts and colors: ²/₃ yard red, ½ yard off-white, ¼ yard gold
- [ ] green yarn for pom-poms
- [ ] 1½×4-inch piece of heavy cardboard (a box scrap)
- [ ] ²/₃ yard satin cord for the hanger

the pearly greats

❧ Members of the Victorian Pearlies, a London charitable group dating back to 1875, covered their clothing with white buttons. This velvet-cuffed wool stocking nods to the pearly craft.

1 Enlarge the pattern on *page 155* to scale, adding ½-inch seam allowances to the sides. Cut a stocking front and back from wool. With right sides facing, sew the front to the back, leaving the top edge open. Clip the curves, trim the seam allowances, and turn the stocking to the right side.

2 Cut a 13-inch-wide band of velvet long enough to go around the top for the cuff, adding ½-inch seam allowances to the ends. With right sides facing, join the short ends. Fold the cuff in half so the long raw edges match and wrong sides are facing. Machine-baste along the raw edges.

3 Using black thread, sew white buttons to the cuff. Slip the cuff inside the top of the stocking so the buttons face the wrong side of the stocking. Align the raw edges of the stocking and the cuff and sew around the top edge. Turn the cuff to the outside and down over the stocking.

4 Fold the cord in half and knot each end with an overhand knot. Sew each knot to the inside of the stocking along the seam line, forming a double-strand hanging cord.

nordic treasures

❧ Pointed knit hats tipped with pom-poms are the inspiration for a felt jester stocking that brings to mind fun times and warm memories.

1 Enlarge the pattern on *page 154* to scale. Cut out a complete red front and back. Cut two top bands and a cuff from off-white. Cut one bottom band from gold.

2 On the stocking front, pin the gold bottom band in place over the stocking. Zigzag along all the gold edges. Lay both off-white upper bands over the stocking front and zigzag them in place along all edges. These multiple layers will give extra body to the stocking top so it hangs better.

3 Working from the wrong side, trim most of the red felt away from under the gold felt. This will help eliminate bulk when turning the stocking. With right sides facing, lay the stocking back over the stocking front and sew them together leaving the top edge open. Clip the curves, trim the seams, and turn the stocking right side out.

4 Turn one end of the cuff under ¾ inch and topstitch it in place using zigzag stitches. With wrong sides facing, sew the ends of the cuff together. Fold the cuff in half crosswise so the raw edges meet. Lightly press.

5 Slip the cuff over the stocking so the hem of the cuff aligns with the bottom of the off-white band and the fold aligns with the top edge. Pin the inner cuff to the inside of

the stocking. Turn the stocking wrong side out and slip-stitch the cuff to the stocking.

6 To make the pom-poms, wind yarn around the cardboard 75 times. Pack the yarn tightly for a fuller pom-pom. After the yarn is wrapped, slip another strand of yarn between the loops and cardboard at any spot. Tie the yarn very tightly in a single knot. Slip the yarn off the cardboard. Pull the knot as tightly as possible and secure it with a second knot. Clip the loops opposite the knot so the yarn releases into a pom-pom. Fluff the pom-pom and trim it with scissors to be as circular as possible. Repeat to make six pom-poms. Tack five pom-poms to the lower edge of the cuff, spacing them evenly. Tack the remaining pom-pom to the toe.

7 Tie a knot in each end of the hanging loop. Sew each knot to the inside of the stocking at the seam line.

What You'll Need...

- [ ] 1 yard boiled wool
- [ ] boiled wool scraps in various colors
- [ ] compass or circle templates
- [ ] yarn
- [ ] large-eye darning needle
- [ ] ½ yard jumbo rickrack

lucky pennies

❧ This long and lean stocking is a spin-off on the penny rug. Disks of wool felt stack one on the other and are joined with embroidery stitches in a similar fashion to how the rugs are made.

1 Enlarge the stocking pattern on *page 155* to scale, adding ½-inch seam allowances to the sides. Cut a front and a back from the boiled wool fabric.

2 Arrange the wool scraps into four groups of three each, mixing the colors as desired. From each set cut a 4¾-inch circle, a 3½-inch circle, and a 1¾-inch circle.

3 Center the small circles over the medium circles and sew them in place with yarn using long stitches or blanket stitches. Repeat for the medium circles, centering them on the large circles. Starting about 3½ inches from the top, sew a circle stack to the center of the stocking. Repeat with the other circles, spacing them about ½ inch apart. See the photograph *above* for details.

4 With right sides facing and using ½-inch seam allowances, sew the stocking front to the stocking back, leaving the top edge open. Clip the curves, trim the seams, and turn the stocking to the right side.

5 Turn under the upper 1½ inches of the stocking. Using long stitches, sew the hem in place. Knot the ends of the rickrack and sew them to the inside of the stocking at the seam lines to create a hanger.

little houses

Collectible ornaments and a simple color palette help
make holiday decorating a snap.

It's often said that less is more, and that thought can apply to holiday decorating. Using a single theme and keeping the froufrou to a minimum often give more impact to a collection. Here miniature cardboard houses are the central theme. The houses, which are reproductions of ornaments made in the '20s and '30s, blend well with the home's vintage furniture. Shades of green provide a gentle background for the little village.

tiny town

A flowerpot and inverted bowls elevate a few houses in this little town, *opposite*, making each one more visible. The houses used here are all the same scale, while the ones on the tree at *right* vary in size. Although these houses are made of cardboard, the idea would work for any type of village collection, easily creating hills and dales for a little burg.

a bit of history

Small cardboard houses and buildings are one of the new holiday collectibles among antiques lovers. Most of the vintage village pieces were made in Japan in the 1920s and 1930s, although some were manufactured as late as the 1950s. The buildings were known for details such as bottlebrush trees, little fences, gingerbread edging, and cellophane doors and windows. Mica powder often was used to add sparkle or snow, giving the ornaments the nickname "mica houses."

Larger buildings generally had a hole in the back to accommodate a lightbulb so the cellophane windows and doors took on a colorful glow when lit. Smaller versions were more likely to have a hanging loop.

village christmas tree

A tree hung with tiny houses, churches, and other buildings has the appearance of a little village set on a mountainside. A ribbon garland mimics winding roadways. Many such ornaments have an opening in the back for tree lights, allowing the village to be illuminated at night. Look for reproduction houses in Christmas departments. They often sport the same detail as their original counterparts but without the wear and tear. Some are available as collections so the scale is the same and the colors coordinate. Vintage houses and buildings can be found at antiques shops, flea markets, and online auctions.

"barrowed" space

❧ An antique toy wheelbarrow filled with ornaments gives a holiday touch to a country cupboard. A small swag of greens and a few wrapped packages are the only other items it takes to transform the cupboard from its daily decor to one filled with Christmas spirit.

nesting instincts

❧ A crystal candlestick takes the place of a nest for a felt bird ornament. For an easy centerpiece, place several bird ornaments on squatty candlesticks. Surround them with taller candlesticks with tapers and a scattering of miniature Christmas ornaments.

picture perfect

❧ Layered frames are a unique way to give impact to a small item. When the frames match the wall color, the ornament comes into sharp focus. Simply hang a large frame on the wall, then suspend a smaller one in the center using wide ribbon. Tuck a swag of greens under the ribbon along the edge of the top frame and tie the ornament to the bow that holds the small frame.

the second time around

Rescue worn, scratched, or slightly damaged ornaments with ribbons and other trims.

Vintage ornaments may take on a warm patina as they age, but modern-day ones often look tacky after just a few seasons. Spiff them up by disguising their flaws with simple crafts store embellishments.

seeing spots

🐛 Surface dents marred this plastic ball *right,* giving it a pockmarked look. Turn those dimples into a fun polka-dot pattern. Hot-glue split peas over the dents, then add more to cover the ball in dots. (Small rhinestone gems or beads also would work.) Add a matching ribbon to the hanger.

give it a swirl

🐛 Color is what saved this orb *left* from the trash can, but some of that color had chipped off, exposing the silver base. Make the silver a part of the design by adding even more. Apply hot glue to the ball in a swirling pattern and let it cool. Peel off the glue to reveal a silver swirl pattern. Add a second swirl of glue in a different pattern and carefully press small silver bead garland into the glue before it cools. Add a loop of garland to the top for a hanger.

43

who's who

🐛 Ornaments that were a trendy color one year may look dated a few years later. Add a splash of color and some personality by painting on a name or other decorations. Purple updates the plain pale ornament *below* with a palette that's more current. Using a purchased stencil and acrylic paint, add a name, holiday greeting, or festive design. Add a bow to the top.

the velvet touch

🐛 This pretty pink ornament *opposite* has a fresh Victorian look but once sported scratches from improper storage. Bands of velvet ribbon now hide the scratches and make the ball look better than ever. Cut three pieces of ribbon to fit around the ball from the cap to the bottom and back to the cap. Hot-glue the ribbon at equidistant intervals to form six stripes that cover the scratches. Cut six smaller pieces of ribbon and shape them into loops. Glue the loops to the top between the stripes so they drape over the ball. Fold additional ribbon into a multiloop bow and glue it to the top.

flirty skirting

🌀 Bands of ribbon saved this cracked ornament *left* from being tossed aside. Cut ⅝-inch-wide ribbon into 1½- and 2-inch lengths. Starting at the bottom, hot-glue three rows of the shorter strips to the ball so it is covered by a skirt of ribbon. Working your way up, glue rows of the longer ribbon to the middle and top of the ball. Trim the ribbon to the desired length, if needed, so the ribbons flip out flapper style.

all that glitters

🌀 The original red and bright gold colors of this plastic ornament *right* were too bright for a tree that had gone from garish to glamorous. Spray the ball with two coats of matte silver paint. Brush thick crafts glue along one swirl and press the glue into a bowlful of silver seed beads. Repeat with every other swirl, letting the glue dry between applications. Add a silver bow to the top.

snow easy

🌀 Clear glass ornaments beg to have decorations either inside or outside their sparkling shell—this one *left* has both. Using paper rolled into a funnel, fill the orb half full of artificial snow, then replace the cap. Adhere silvery snowflake decals from a scrapbooking store or department to the outside, gently pressing and forming them to the rounded sides. Add small beaded garland to the top.

getting ruffled

~ Fluorescent yellow looked great on a funky-
style tree years ago but was a bit too jarring for today's
decor. Lightly coat the surface *above* with green
acrylic paint and let it dry. Add a second coat of paint.
While the paint is still wet, gently rub some of it away
for a mottled look. Cut wide wire-edge ribbon two
to three times the circumference of the ball. On one
long edge of the ribbon, pull the wire to gather that
side and form a ribbon ruffle. Do not remove the
wire from either side. Glue the ruffle to the top of
the ornament and trim away the excess wire. Shape
the outer edge into pretty flounces. If the cap is also
unattractive, spray-paint it before replacing it.

What You'll Need...

- [ ] thin cardboard (about the weight of a mailing box)
- [ ] sharp crafts knife and a cutting surface
- [ ] pencil
- [ ] light pink cotton fabric
- [ ] tacky glue
- [ ] disposable foam brushes
- [ ] ultra-fine (size 000) permanent marking pen
- [ ] red pencil or permanent marking pen
- [ ] pink powdered blush and small paintbrush (optional)
- [ ] heavy watercolor paper
- [ ] raw umber acrylic paint
- [ ] artist's paintbrush
- [ ] silver and gold high-quality artist's glitter (see *page 158* for suggested brands)
- [ ] 1/3 yard ivory satin for the angel's skirt
- [ ] hot-glue gun and glue sticks
- [ ] scraps of curly yarn for hair
- [ ] scrap of 5/8-inch-wide beige velvet ribbon
- [ ] 1/2 yard gold cording
- [ ] scrap of old jewelry for the necklace
- [ ] seed pearls
- [ ] 22-gauge silver-color wire
- [ ] 6–8 assorted beads
- [ ] heavy off-white thread
- [ ] thin cord for hanging

angels on high

A host of Heaven's best is ready to watch over one and all.

peaceful olivia

An angel wall hanging wears wings that resemble an olive branch, spreading a message of hope and peace.

1 Enlarge the patterns on *page 156* to scale. Using a crafts knife, cut the body from cardboard. Trace the upper body and leg patterns onto pink fabric. Lightly draw the face onto the upper body piece. Cut out the fabric pieces.

2 Brush tacky glue onto the cardboard upper body and legs. Smooth the matching fabric pieces over the cardboard pieces. Clip from the fabric edge up to the cardboard. Turn the fabric margins to the back and glue down.

3 After the glue dries, draw the face with the fine marker. Make a small red dot for the lips. If desired, brush the cheeks with blush. Set the body aside.

4 Cut two wings from watercolor paper. Paint both sides of each wing raw umber. Let dry. Paint the wing fronts again. While the paint is wet, sprinkle generously with glitter. After the paint dries, shake off the excess glitter. If the wings are not rigid enough, hot-glue a strand of wire to the back. Set aside.

5 Cut the skirt shaper from cardboard. Cut two skirt pieces from satin. Pin the pieces together, right sides facing. Using a 1/4-inch seam allowance, sew along the top and both sides. Turn right side out and press lightly. Hand- or machine-baste the bottom edges together.

6 Tear a piece of silk 1 inch wide by the width of the fabric. Sew a running stitch down the middle of the torn strip. Gather the strip to fit the bottom of the skirt and knot the gathering thread. Handsew or hot-glue the gathered strip to the hem of the skirt. Take another running stitch along the skirt top and gather it to fit the waist of the body. Knot the gathering thread ends.

7 Lay the skirt over the cardboard skirt shaper, taking care that the cardboard is covered at the bottom edge. Pin the sides in place, leaving enough fabric to wrap to the back of the cardboard. Place the center of the gathered waist at the center top marking. Hot-glue the skirt to the shaper at the waist and bottom corners. Glue the skirt sides to the back.

8 Tear a 1×4-inch piece of fabric for the bodice and ravel one long edge. Gather the opposite edge to fit the waist. Glue the bodice to the body at the waist. Glue the skirt and skirt shaper in place.

9 Cut three 8-inch lengths of yarn for the hair. Glue the hair in place and trim to the desired length. Dip the ends in tacky glue to prevent fraying. Let the glue dry.

10 Hot-glue the velvet ribbon to the waist. Wrap gold roping over the ribbon and tie it at the front. Tack the cord in place with hot glue. Knot the ends.

11 Trim the necklace scrap to fit the neck and glue it in place.

12 Thread the pearls onto the wire. Shape the wire into a 2 1/2-inch-diameter circle for the halo. Hot-glue the halo in place on the back of the head.

13 Hot-glue the wings to the back.

14 For the garland, cut a small slit or make a small hole in each hand. String the beads onto the thread. Slip the thread ends through the hand slits and hot-glue the ends to the back.

15 Cut the hanging cord to the desired length. Tie the cord around the wings.

- medium-weight high-quality watercolor paper
- small sharp scissors or a crafts knife and self-healing cutting mat
- gold and burnt umber artist's watercolor in a tube
- flat 1/2-inch watercolor brush
- smooth foam-core board (available at art stores)
- spray glue for paper
- 3/16-inch-wide brown grosgrain ribbon (stretchable if available)
- hot-glue gun and glue sticks
- head pin
- small beads and one faceted crystal
- 5-inch ivory column candle
- 1 package of 3/16-inch brass nailheads (available at crafts stores in the wearable art department)
- small glass candleholder

48

praying pair

❧ The Christmas blessing is conveyed in a gold painted and cut-paper altarpiece that glows warmly in the candlelight.

1 Enlarge the pattern on *page 154* to scale. Trace the angel pattern onto watercolor paper and carefully cut out the background areas, leaving only the shaded angels, star, and outer arch.

2 Paint the cut paper burnt umber using very little water so the color is smooth and even. Let dry.

3 Lay the pattern on the foam-core board and trace and cut around the perimeter. Paint the foam-core board gold using very little water so the surface is smooth and even.

4 Lightly score a line down the vertical center of the foam-core board. Make the same score line on the angels, going through the arch, star, hands, and base. Fit the angels over the foam-core board and make any necessary adjustments in the fit of the outer edges. Fold both pieces slightly toward the center.

5 Join the angels to the foam-core board with spray glue. Hot-glue ribbon to the outer edges but not the bottom. String the beads onto the head pin. Press the end of the head pin through the center of the star and bend it down at the back.

6 Gently press the nailheads into the candle in an even pattern. Place the candle in the candleholder and set it in front of the diptych. Keep the candle a safe distance from the diptych and never leave a burning candle unattended.

angel joy

❧ A wire angel dressed in lace spreads the joy of the season when clipped onto a lamp, tree, or valance.

NOTE: If rust-color wire is not available at crafts or hardware stores, use another wire in the same gauge and sand it with steel wool. After the body is completely shaped, paint the wire brown.

1 Cut the wire into a 20-inch length for the body and a 6-inch length for the arms. Set the arm piece aside.

2 To shape the body, fold the 20-inch wire in half over a 1/2-inch-diameter dowel. Twist the wire on itself for 5/8 inch to form the neck and torso. Draw the legs down and trim them to 5 1/2 inches. Sand the cut edges to remove any burrs or rough spots.

- 26 inches of 14–16-gauge rust-color wire (see other options *below*)
- wire cutters
- ½-inch-diameter dowel, paintbrush handle, or kitchen tool handle
- fine sandpaper
- 24–28-gauge florist's wire
- hot-glue gun and glue sticks
- acrylic paint in dark brown and ivory
- 1¼-inch wooden star (available at crafts stores)
- 7/16-inch flat white button with two holes
- paintbrush
- silver and gold high-quality glitter (see *page 158* for suggested brands)
- ultra-fine-tip red permanent marker
- two 1½-inch pieces of sparse silk evergreen
- 4×10½-inch piece of delicate net-style lace
- needle and thread
- ⅓ yard narrow gold ribbon
- alligator clip (available at hardware stores)

49

3 Center the arm wire across the body at the end of the twisting. Sash it in place with the florist's wire. Add a dot of hot glue to secure. Cut the arms to 2½ inches each; sand the ends.

4 Shape the wires so the arms curve up, the left leg bows very slightly, and the right leg bends out at the knee. See the photograph *above right* for details. Dip the tips of the hands and the left leg in ivory paint. Set aside.

5 To form the head, center the button on the wooden star and trace around it. Remove the button. Paint the front and sides of the star brown. Do not paint inside the button outline. Paint a second coat. While the paint is still wet, sprinkle it with glitter. After the paint dries, shake off the excess glitter.

6 To make the face, run a piece of narrow florist's wire through one button hole from front to back. Bring the wire back to the front through the other hole. Bend the wire to the back of the button and trim the ends short. This will form a line from each "eye" to the outer edge of the button and make it appear that the button is wired to the star. Using the red marker, draw a small heart for the mouth. Glue the button to the star.

7 Trim the evergreen pieces so half of each piece is stem only. Using florist's wire, attach the evergreen wings to the angel where the arms join the body. Add a dot of hot glue to the back if needed. See the photograph *above* for details.

8 Sew a running stitch along one long edge of the lace. Draw up the lace into gathers using the stitching. Wrap the skirt around the body just below the arms and use the thread ends to wrap and tie the skirt to the body. Add hot glue if needed. Tie the gold ribbon over the gathering. Trim the ribbon ends.

9 Hot glue the head over the wire head loop. If desired, paint and glitter the back of the head. Take care not to get glitter in the wings and skirt.

10 Wrap the right foot with thread to make it thicker. Hot-glue the right foot into the alligator clip. NOTE: Epoxy or industrial-strength glue (such as Beacon Quick Grip) can be used to attach the alligator clip to the foot.

- ☐ ⅓ yard unbleached muslin
- ☐ polyester fiberfill
- ☐ bamboo sticks, twigs, or small dowels for the arms and legs
- ☐ small saw to cut the arms and legs
- ☐ drill with small bit
- ☐ acrylic paint in brown, medium olive green, and turquoise
- ☐ silver and gold high-quality glitter (see page 158 for suggested brands)
- ☐ embossed cardstock
- ☐ tacky glue
- ☐ ivory quilting thread and long needle
- ☐ scrap of aluminum flashing or other thin sheet metal
- ☐ heavy duty scissors or crafting tin snips
- ☐ fine sandpaper
- ☐ hammer and center punch
- ☐ 1-inch button with two holes for the face
- ☐ scrap of new or vintage eyelet for the outer skirt
- ☐ scrap of fine lace or tulle for the underskirt
- ☐ hot-glue gun and glue sticks
- ☐ 1 yard ¼-inch-wide ribbon
- ☐ chenille strip

50

angelica in buttons and bows

❧ This little angel is sweetly feminine with a lace skirt, button face, and tiny silk bows tied to her glittered arms and legs.

1 Enlarge the patterns on *page 156* to scale. Trace the body pattern onto muslin. With right sides facing, sew through two layers of muslin along the stitching lines. Leave the bottom edge open for stuffing. Cut out the body piece ¼ inch beyond the stitching line. Clip the curves. Turn, stuff, and sew the bottom edge closed. Set the body aside.

2 Cut two 4½-inch sticks for the arms and two 9-inch sticks for the legs. Drill a hole through one end of each arm and leg piece. Paint the arms and legs brown; let dry. Paint again and while still wet, sprinkle with glitter. After the paint dries, shake off the excess glitter. Set aside.

3 To make the wings, glue two pieces of textured cardstock back-to-back. Trace the wing pattern onto the paper and cut out. Using a needle, make four small holes at the center of the wings as marked on the pattern. Paint the front and back of the wings turquoise; let dry. Using your finger, gently rub olive paint across the raised surfaces of the paper; let dry. Set aside.

4 For the star halo, trace the star onto the metal and cut out. Using a center punch, tap dot patterns onto the star. Drill four small holes in the center of the star.

5 Using a double strand of heavy thread, sew the arms and legs to the body at the upper and lower corners. Use loose stitches so the limbs move freely.

6 Sew a button to the head for the face. Use a long needle and go all the way through the head with the stitches.

7 Cut a 7×24-inch piece of vintage eyelet for the outer skirt and an 8×24-inch piece of lace for the underskirt. With right sides facing, sew the short ends of the eyelet together. Turn right side out and sew running stitches along the top edge for gathers. Repeat for the underskirt.

8 Place the underskirt on the body as marked on the pattern. Draw up the gathers and sew the underskirt to the body. Repeat for the overskirt.

9 Position the halo on the back of the head and mark the holes. Remove the halo and take a backstitch at each dot, leaving long tails of threads. Run the threads through the holes in the halo and tie the halo to the head. Secure with a dot of hot glue between the head and halo.

10 Sew and glue the wings to the back of the angel in the same manner.

11 Cut the ribbon into four pieces. Tie a bow at each shoulder and ankle. Trim the ends to the desired length.

12 Shape the chenille strip into a 1-inch-diameter circle; cut away the excess. Sew the circle to the back of the angel for hanging on the tree.

serene in green

A home filled with warm light and quieted with a single-color palette holds a sense of peace and sanctuary in a season of chaos.

textural
touches

✎ Embossed bowls filled
with ornaments *opposite* join
holly and candles on a window
seat where nature's earthy
elements are brightened
by little touches of sparkle
that catch both daylight and
candlelight.

all is calm

✎ Nature gives the cue in
a gently colored room.
Colors as soft as moss,
soothing as sage, and rich as
emerld mingle with all
shades of white.
A fir tree *right* that brushes
the ceiling is packed with satin
and shiny balls in graduated
sizes. Hundreds of glass icicles
and yard after yard of gold
package cord add sparkle
to the tree.

gentle touches

A garland of pleated ribbon forms a band of color between natural linen stockings and a white mantel. Tall topiaries and a wreath of mixed greens bring elements of nature to the setting.

ribbon garland

1. Thread the needle with the string or cord. Use enough for the entire length of the garland if possible.

2. Accordion pleat the ribbon at 3-inch intervals, leaving a long tail at each end. Run the needle through the center of the pleats.

3. When the garland fills the string, tie off the string at each end so the knot forms a hanging loop. Trim the ribbon ends to a 45-degree angle.

linen and lace stockings

1. Enlarge the pattern on *page 155* to scale. Cut out the stocking front and back, adding ¹⁄₂-inch seam allowances all around.

2. Sew the laces to the stocking front, leaving the top 2 inches of the stocking free from lace. Trim the laces even with the stocking at the sides.

3. Using a zipper foot, machine-baste the cording to the stocking front so the edge of the cording aligns with the seam line. Do not apply cording to the top edge of the stocking.

4. With right sides facing, sew the stocking front to the stocking back, leaving the upper edge open. Narrowly hem the upper edge. Trim the seam allowances, clip the curves, and turn the stocking right side out.

5. Fold the upper 1¹⁄₂ inches of the stocking to the inside and press. Topstitch along the folded edge. For the hanger, fold the ribbon in half crosswise to form a loop. Sew the loop to the inside of the stocking at the upper right corner.

soft as snow

Fleecy mittens pinned on a string form a garland for a mantel lined with pinecones and moss-filled pots.

fleecy mitten garland

1. Enlarge the mitten pattern on *page 155* to scale. For each mitten, cut a front and a back. Pin the mittens together with wrong sides facing and machine-zigzag along the edges to join the two pieces. Leave the top edge open. Repeat for each pair of mittens.

2. Drape the twine under the mantel, allowing the ends to hang freely. Attach the mittens to the twine with miniature clothespins. Trim the twine as desired.

55

simple in style

Keeping patterns and colors to a minimum reduces the visual clutter that is so common at Christmas. A napkin with a hint of plaid offers up the only pattern on a linen-covered table. Tie the napkin with ribbon, then tuck a sprig of silk holly between the two.

pastoral pasture

Flats of grass serve as a centerpiece and bring reminders of spring throughout the room. Just for fun, a pair of metal cows grazes near the tabletop pasture. Grow the grass a few weeks ahead of time by planting wheat grass seeds in a plastic-lined box. Health food stores, garden shops, and florists may have flats of grass available for purchase.

warm welcome

✎ A little clutch of greens tucked into natural wool mittens welcomes friends and family. Pin purchased mittens to wide ribbons, then slip holly and evergreen sprigs into them. Pin the other end of the ribbons to the narrow top edge of the door with a flat tack.

packing up

This year, instead of hunting for the right size
boxes and bags, make your own.

Forget scrounging in the basement for a make-do box or popping for expensive gift bags. Use decorative cardstock to make pillow- or tote-style boxes to fit hard-to-disguise gifts such as CDs, bottles, and gift cards. For bags, choose the inexpensive patterned or solid lunch bag style. The key is to add unusual embellishments so the container is almost a gift in itself.

TO MAKE A SHALLOW PILLOW-STYLE BOX

Cut the pattern on *page 157* from cardstock, adjusting the size to fit your gift. For an extra-large box, use lightweight poster board. Cover one side with wrapping paper, using spray glue to join the paper and poster board.

Using a crafts knife and straightedge, lightly score a line $1/2$ inch from one long edge. Fold the edge over so wrong sides match. Score another line parallel to the first and halfway between the fold and the opposite edge. Fold the paper along the second scoring, wrong sides facing. Apply quick-drying tacky crafts glue under the folded flap and tuck the opposite edge under the flap to create a pocket. Run a brayer or rolling pin over the joint.

After the glue dries, lightly score an arc along each open edge. Use the pattern on *page 157* as a guide, adjusting it to fit your box. Fold the curved edges in, creating a pillow-style box.

go retro

Funky colors, prints, and shapes reminiscent of the 60s give a hot retro look to packages. Close the box with a single band of ribbon. Add a gift tag cut from coordinating paper. For the bag, make a tag by layering strips of white cardstock and two decorative papers. Hand-letter or stamp a holiday greeting at the end of the white cardstock. Fold the tag over so the

greeting is exposed. See the photograph *opposite* for details.

Fold down the upper edge of the bag and align the fold of the tag with the edge of the bag, centering the tag. Punch two holes through all layers. Run narrow ribbon through the holes from back to front. Hold a sputnik-style ornament over the tag and tie it in place with the ribbon.

TO MAKE A TOTE-STYLE BOX

Cut the pattern on *page 155* from mat board, adjusting the size to fit your gift. Score the lines as indicated on the pattern, adjusting them as needed to fit your gift. Cut out the rectangular openings. Punch holes as indicated on the pattern.

Fold the sides up along the scored lines. Place the bottle in the box. Using thin but sturdy cord, start at the front and thread one end of the cord through one bottom hole and the other end through the other bottom hole. Wrap the cord around the bottle to hold it in place and bring the ends out the bottom holes in the back. Cross the cord at the back of the container, forming an X. Run the cord ends through

the top holes, around the bottle neck, and through the front holes. See the photograph *above left* for details. Tie the ends so the bottle is secure in the box.

Wrap narrow cord around the top edge to strengthen the handle. Bring the ends to the front and tie in a knot or bow. See the photograph *above* for details.

be fruitful

Give a decanter tote a lush look with sugared fruits. Glue and wire artificial sugared fruits to the front of the tote. Add snippets of ribbon and wire or twig coils if desired.

TO MAKE A DEEP TWO-PIECE PILLOW-STYLE GIFT BOX

✍ Cut a top and bottom from cardstock using the pattern on *page 157*, adjusting the size to fit your gift. For an extra-large box, use lightweight poster board and cover it with wrapping paper, using spray glue to adhere the wrapping paper to the poster board.

Using a crafts knife, lightly score along all the curved lines as indicated on the pattern. Fold in the arcs and fit one piece over the other to form a box. See the photograph *left* for details. Hold the pieces together with a ribbon.

red hot

✍ Add a touch of cheer to your gifts this year with bright red and clean white wrappings. For the box, wrap a red pillow box with wide sheer ribbon. Before tying the bow, slip a small ornament onto the ribbon. For the bag, cut a long narrow tag (about 2×9 inches) from red cardstock; center a slightly smaller piece of white cardstock over it and glue them together. Stamp the white layer with a holiday greeting. Glue a red satin ribbon under the tag. Fold the tag onto itself 2 inches from the unstamped edge.

Fold the upper edge of the bag down. Punch a hole $3/4$ inch in from each outer edge, placing one hole slightly higher than the other. Thread a 14-inch length of cord through each hole, forming two loops on the front. Slide a candy cane through the loops and tie the cord in bows on the back. Slip the card behind the candy cane so the fold of the card lays on the top of the bag.

gentle flurries

A snowflake-covered box blankets a CD, softening its form like a fresh coat of snow rounds out the shapes of nature. Decorate the box by punching snowflake shapes from white self-adhesive seals and decorative papers. Stick and glue the snowflakes to the box. Add a few small jewels for a bit of sparkle. Tie the box closed with sheer ribbon.

jeweled box

Some boxes are just too pretty to toss. Cover any labels or blank surfaces with decorative paper, using spray adhesive to join the paper to the box. Using an awl, punch a hole in the center of the box top. Add an eyelet. To make the dangling beads, fold a length of cord in half and make an overhand knot at the folded end. String gems onto a head pin. Run the end of the head pin through the knot, bend it back on itself, and trim away any excess length. Run the other ends of the cord through the hole in the box lid. Knot the cord on the back of the lid so the fob dangles at the desired length.

oh, christmas trees

Simplified trees add a bit of gaiety to a deep pillow package and a bag tied with mittens. For the box, cut a simple triangular tree shape from decorative paper. Adhere flat-sided jewels to the tree, using a star-shape jewel for the top. Add a narrow trunk to the bottom, gluing it to the back of the tree. Cut contrasting paper into a narrow ribbon. Wrap the paper ribbon around the box and glue the ends at the box back. Attach the tree decoration to the box using self-adhesive foam dots.

For the bag, purchase a large single tree-shape sticker. Cut a piece of cardstock to fit the sticker. Cut a contrasting piece of cardstock slightly larger. Glue the two pieces together, centering them. Cut a piece of foam-core board the same size as the cardstock. Glue the cardstock pieces to the foam-core board. Center the sticker on the cardstock. Glue the foam-core board to the bag. Glue furry trim around the edge of the foam-core board.

Fold over the top of the bag. Punch two holes near the center of the bag just below the fold line. Run a cord through the holes from back to front and tie it in a knot at center front. Trim the ends to the desired length. Using the pattern on *page 155*, cut four mittens from the contrasting cardstock. Glue two mittens to each end of the cord, sandwiching the cord between the mittens. Glue fur trim to the edge of the mittens.

▶ Study in Contrast
Tiny pinecones, silver balls, and miniature prisms mix it up in a shallow silver bowl. The contrast between the rustic natural pinecones and the sparkling balls and prisms is intriguing and makes both elements more interesting.

In a Twinkling

decorating

◀ Starry, Starry Sight
To get the most display power out of a small collection, fill a sleigh, bowl, or other holiday vessel with ornaments of a similar color and shape. Here crystal, gold, and silver stars are piled in a silver sleigh. The collection has more impact when clustered together than it would if it was spread out on a tree.

▼ Music to the Eyes CDs, with their iridescent, shimmering look, form a backdrop for inexpensive snowflake ornaments. Use clear industrial-strength glue (available at crafts stores) to attach one or more glittered snowflake ornaments to the plain side of a blank or advertisement CD. To form the garland, snip bead garland into short pieces. Using a double strand of thread, tie one end of the garland to the tip of a snowflake. Continue until the entire strand is formed. If the CDs tip forward when hung, tape coins to the back along the lower edge until they stay upright.

▲ The Lights Fantastic
Old and new chandelier crystals sparkle richly when hung from a wire tree. Originally meant to show off ornaments, the open tree allows the crystals to hang freely and catch the light. Add some crystal garlands to fill in the empty spaces between spirals.

63

◀ Bowl of Baubles
For a super-simple decoration, gather up a few strands of garlands, a candle, and a low footed bowl. Place a pillar candle in the center of the bowl. If needed, secure it with florist's clay or sticky candle adhesive. Fill the remainder of the bowl with several strands of garlands. Clip S-shape ornament hooks over the rim of the bowl and swag two or more garlands around the bowl from hook to hook.

of friends. Take time to appreciate the one thing you hold closest to your heart—your friends and family. Welcome guests into your home with warm food, cool drinks, rich desserts, and casual entertaining. Host a party inspired by a French bistro or invite everyone into the kitchen to share an evening of cooking and feasting.

GATHERING *together*

paisley
point of
view

Paint plain glass dinnerware with the pattern that is both timeless and trendy—paisley.

paisley is back

Like an old friend, paisley never goes away but rather comes back for a welcomed visit from time to time. Invite the pattern to your dinner table by handpainting a simplified version of the classic design in updated colors. Glass paint that's cured in the oven is permanent and dishwasher safe.

the center of it all

❧ Keeping the centerpiece *opposite* low and simple lets the dinnerware take a starring role. A long, narrow tray is first lined with silk leaves and fuchsia ornaments, then clusters of gold berries are tucked in for a slightly formal look.

three-dot napkins

❧ A trio of buttons decorates one corner of the purchased napkin. Gold seed beads are sewn on with the same stitch that attaches the button to the napkin. Make sure both the buttons and beads are washable.

1 Using three strands of embroidery floss, sew a small button to the place mat, placing it 1¾ inches in from the lower right corner and 1 inch up from the bottom edge. On the final stitch through the button, slip a gold seed bead onto the needle and floss so it is centered over the button.

2 Add two small buttons, a large button, and another small button in a straight line above the first button. Space the small buttons 1 inch apart; leave 1½ inches between the large button and the small button on each side of it. See the photograph at *right* for details. Sew all the buttons in the same manner as the first one, slipping a seed bead onto the last stitch.

3 Sew a circle of seed beads around the large button. See the photograph at *right* for details. Repeat for each place mat.

4 For the napkin, sew three buttons (each with a center seed bead) in one corner of the napkin, leaving 1 inch of space between the buttons and the napkin edge. Repeat for each napkin.

What You'll Need...

- ☐ purchased napkins and place mats (faux suede are shown)
- ☐ ½-inch- and ¾-inch-diameter red buttons
- ☐ red embroidery floss
- ☐ needle
- ☐ large gold seed beads

all buttoned up

❧ A row of buttons added to a purchased place mat mimics the rows of dots on the dinnerware. Gold seed beads add sparkle to each of the buttons.

What You'll Need...

- [ ] clear glass plates and plain tumblers
- [ ] vinegar
- [ ] clean, lint-free cloths
- [ ] disposable plate or other paint palette
- [ ] glass paint in white, red, metallic gold, pine green, and magenta
- [ ] small round and flat artist's paintbrushes
- [ ] masking tape
- [ ] pencil with new eraser
- [ ] thick rubber bands

70

GENERAL INSTRUCTIONS

1 Wash the plates and glasses in warm, soapy water. Rinse, then wipe with vinegar and dry. This will remove any residue that may keep the paint from bonding. During the painting process, take care when handling the dishes so your fingers do not transfer oil or residue to the glassware.

2 Enlarge the patterns on *page 154* to scale or to fit your plate. Make enough photocopies for each plate and tumbler. Cut out the plate patterns to fit the plate and cut out the individual designs for the tumblers.

3 Shake all the paint well. Mix white paint with pine green to get light green and with red to get pink. Squirt dabs of each color paint onto the paper plate.

4 Paint according to the directions following. After the paint dries, bake the tumblers and inverted plates according to the paint manufacturer's directions.

FOR EACH PLATE

NOTE: The plates are painted from the underneath side.

1 Tape the pattern to the right side of the plate with the print facing down so you can see the pattern's design through the plate when looking at the back side.

2

For the large paisley, dip the brush handle into green paint and make the dots that outline the paisley. Repeat using white for the partial paisley, pink for the small paisley, and gold for the circles. Use

a pencil eraser to make the large dots. See the photograph *below left* for details.

3 Paint the strokes in the center of each paisley using red in the large paisley, pink in the small paisley, and magenta in the partial paisley. See the photograph *top left* for details. Let the paint dry completely.

4 Fill in the background of the paisleys, painting over the brushstrokes to the center of the dotted outlines. See the photograph *above* for details.

colorful dining

Easy brushstrokes and rows of dots form the paisley pattern on clear glass dinnerware and glassware. For safety, the painting is done on the underside of the dinnerware and kept away from the top inch of the glassware's rim. To add color to the background, bright tissue paper is placed between the painted plate and the gold charger.

FOR EACH TUMBLER

NOTE: The tumblers are painted on the outside of the glass.

1 Tape a paisley pattern to the inside of the glass so the design is visible on the outside of the glass. Place a wide rubber band around the glass so it is perfectly level and falls slightly below the center of the paisley pattern.

With a pencil eraser and using the rubber band as a guide, paint red dots around the tumbler and in the center of the circle. Do not paint in the paisley area. Let the paint dry. To ensure that the paint does not run, tip the tumbler from end-to-end every few minutes until the paint is completely set. Let the dots dry.

3 Paint the paisley background white and the circle ring with small gold dots. Let dry.

4 Paint the paisley center red; let dry. Paint small green dots around the paisley. Let dry.

What You'll Need...

- [ ] dark blue, light blue, white, gold, and light yellow cardstock
- [ ] small items to decorate the candle bases: scraps of papers and cardstock, buttons, wire, yarn, frames, eyelets, tacks, Judaic symbols, and other scrapbooking trims (see the photograph *above* for ideas)
- [ ] scissors and specialty cutters such as circle cutters
- [ ] glue and tape
- [ ] 22- to 24-gauge silver wire

welcome to

Open your home this Hanukkah season and let

I nvite friends to share in your family's Hanukkah traditions with a casual gathering on several of the eight nights. Jewish friends will enjoy sharing the fellowship while those of other faiths will be intrigued by the stories, music, games and the lighting of the menorah.

the art of hanukkah

❧ Create a menorah card for the mantel or table from cardstock. Decorate each candle base to be a miniature work of art using scrapbooking trims.

1 Cut five light blue and four dark blue 3×3-inch squares from cardstock. Cut a 3×¾-inch strip of dark blue and tape it to one light square to extend above the square. This will be the shamash (the candle used for lighting the others).

2 Using the card shown *above* as inspiration, decorate each square with the scrapbooking trims and papers.

hanukkah

the light of your friendship burn brightly.

3 Cut nine 1×4-inch rectangles from white for the candles. NOTE: If desired, the shamash candle can be cut slightly larger. Cut nine teardrop shapes from gold for the outer flame and nine small teardrop shapes from light yellow for the inner flames. Glue an inner-flame shape to each outer flame.

4 Glue a candle to the back of each decorated square so 2½ inches extend above the square. Cut the silver wire into 18 pieces, each measuring about 3 inches long. Twist pairs of wire together. Splay out the ends of the wire. Tape one twisted wire to the back of each candle. Glue a flame to the other end of the wire so the wire forms a wick about ¾ inch long.

5 Cut three 2×12-inch-long pieces of dark blue card stock. Fold the pieces accordion style every 3 inches. Glue the strips to the backs of the candles to connect the pieces, placing the shamash at the center. Alternate light and dark blue candle bases along the strip. See the photograph *above* and *opposite* for assembly details.

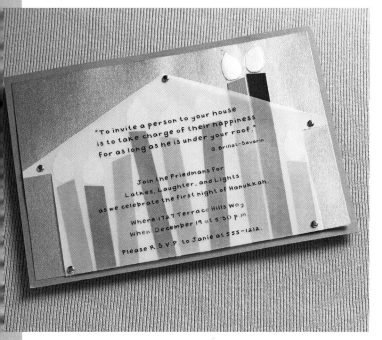

candlelight invitation

ᴥ Invite friends to join you "under your roof" with an invitation that displays the candles and sentiments of Hanukkah.

▌ Using the wording *above* as a guide, print the invitations on vellum using a computer and printer.

▌ Enlarge the house pattern on *page 154* to scale and cut out one house from vellum for a template. Center the template over each printed invitation and trace around it. Cut each printed piece into a house shape.

▌ Cut a 5½×9-inch rectangle of silver cardstock for each invitation. Cut the blue cardstock into long rectangles for candles and the yellow into teardrop shapes for the flames. Glue the candles to the silver rectangles so the lengths and angles of the candles vary. See the photograph *above* for details. Add a flame above each candle.

▌ Center the vellum house over the candles and attach it with mini-brads. Cut blue cardstock slightly larger than the silver cardstock for the backing and glue the invitation to the backing.

What You'll Need...

- [ ] vellum
- [ ] pencil
- [ ] cardstock in silver, yellow, and various shades of blue
- [ ] tape or glue
- [ ] silver mini-brads

gelt box display

ᴥ Little flat boxes hold gelt coin candy for each day of Hanukkah. Line them up on board to make an artistic statement.

▌ Cover the chipboard backing with dark blue cardstock. Cut the light blue cardstock to 11×11 inches. Glue it over the dark blue paper, centering.

▌ Enlarge the box pattern on *page 154* to scale and cut eight boxes from medium blue. Lightly score along the dotted lines with a crafts knife. Decorate each box.

▌ When the box fronts are decorated, fold the cardstock to form flat boxes. Fold the lower flap back and up, and the side flaps back and around to the back. Glue or tape the flaps together at the back, leaving the upper flap free. Center the soft loop side of a self-adhesive hook-and-loop dot on the back of each box.

▌ Cut a piece of white cardstock slightly larger than a box and write a Hanukkah greeting on it. Center it over a piece of medium blue and then dark blue cardstock. Using foam dots, attach it to the center of the backing board. See the photograph *above* for details.

▌ Place the hook side of the hook-and-loop dots on the board in even rows of three, two, and three so the boxes line up evenly. See the photograph *above* for details. Place chocolate gelt or real coins in each box and adhere the boxes to the board with the hook-and-loop tape. If desired, display the board on an easel.

What You'll Need...

- [ ] 12×12-inch piece of chipboard or cardboard
- [ ] light blue, medium blue, dark blue, and white cardstock
- [ ] glue, tape, and self-adhesive foam dots
- [ ] crafts knife
- [ ] various scrapbooking trims to decorate the boxes (see the photograph *above* for inspiration)
- [ ] 8 large self-adhesive dots of hook-and-loop tape
- [ ] easel painted to match the board (optional)

friendly shake

Tiny beads fill a window in each point of this Star of David. When hung on the door or wall, they sparkle in the light. When it's not hung up, the star is a great shaker toy.

1. Enlarge the pattern on *page 155* to scale. Cut two small stars using the inner lines and one large star using the outer lines.

2. Cut the triangles from the six points of one small star and the hexagon from the middle, leaving a skeletal framework. Cut the hexagon from the second small star.

3. Cut acetate triangles to fit over the triangular cutouts and tape them in place on all edges. Place double-sided adhesive foam along the entire skeletal star frame. Do not remove the paper backing. Place beads in each of the points so the space is about two-thirds full. Remove the paper backing from the foam strips and press the second small star over the first one so the beads are fully encased and the edges are sealed.

4. Place double-sided tape along the outer and inner edges of the backing star. Center the shaker star over the large star and press it in place securely.

5. Tear the handmade paper to fit in the hexagonal opening of the small stars. Spell out "Happy Hanukkah" with cording or ribbon and glue it in place, or write it with a white pen. Tape the handmade paper in place. See the photograph *above* for details.

6. Tape a ribbon loop to the back of the star for hanging.

▶ Polka-Dot Parade
Add fun to your table with a Suess-like explosion of dots, curlicues, and fluffy stuff. Paint various-size small wooden disks (available at crafts stores) in bright colors. When they're dry, wrap colorful wire around them, then curl the tail of the wire around a pencil to create a spiral. Make more wire spirals, leaving some tight and stretching others out to be loosely wrapped. Insert the wires into a block of plastic foam. Cover the foam with fluffy white garland, tacking it in place with U-shape pins or hot glue if needed. Add small wire-stemmed ornaments and opened paper clips. Set the centerpiece on a bed of greens.

In a Twinkling
tabletop

◀ In Stitches
Showcase even the most basic embroidery skills on a table runner that is bordered with rolls of colorful felt and oversized stitches. Layer pink and red felt, then fold the long edges up on themselves to form a pink border. Stitch it in place with long running stitches and embroidery floss. On the short ends, roll each layer separately and secure it with large embroidery stitches. Add more rolls of fabric to each end and attach them with straight or diagonal stitches, with large cross-stitches, or by tying.

76

▶ Visions of Sugarplums
For a sweet little centerpiece, fill a silver sugar bowl with a candy-covered tree. Wedge a cone-shape piece of plastic foam tightly into the sugar bowl. Use florist's clay to further secure it if needed. Hot-glue small artificial candied fruits, real or artificial candy, and sprigs of silk greenery to the foam until it is completely covered. Floral picks with candy designs also can be used by inserting the pick into the foam.

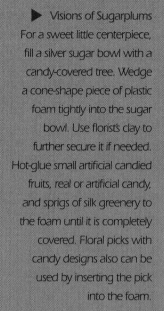

◀ Santa's Bags
Fashion a fast and easy centerpiece from bags even fancier than the one the jolly old elf carries. Wrap packages in gift paper, then tuck them in and around purchased wine or gift bags. Hot-glue silk poinsettias or holly to the bags. To help position the gifts, put some sand in the boxes for weight or wrap blocks of wood instead of boxes.

FIESTA! host a

This year take that collaborative concept of potluck parties one step further by transforming the prep time into party time. Instead of cooking alone, friends can spend time cooking together.

This menu—inspired by the festive and warming flavors of the Southwest—lends itself well to ensemble cooking. It requires a little measuring, mixing, slicing, and dicing, but no tricky techniques. In general, this is the sort of kitchen duty the average cook can pull off while chatting with friends and grooving to good music. What about the non-cooks in your crowd? Put them in charge of the music and games—or the blender.

Invitations with Southwest hues are the first thing to snag your invitees' attentions. Once at your house, aprons you've made as take-home gifts will get everyone in a cook's frame of mind. A party game where the pieces double as coasters will help break the ice. Handpainted glassware and a tile serving tray set the Southwestern mood with color. The resulting party will be fun for everyone, yet easy on you. Who knows? It may change the way you cook and entertain around the holidays.

cooking party
with friends

*Double Apricot
Margaritas*

Double Apricot Margaritas

Lime wedges
Coarse salt
1 15-ounce can unpeeled apricot
    halves, drained
½ cup tequila*
¼ cup sugar
¼ cup lime juice
¼ cup apricot nectar
3 cups ice cubes

Rub lime wedges around rims of
eight frozen margarita glasses or 6-ounce
glasses. Invert glasses into dish of salt to
coat rims. Shake off excess salt. Set aside.

In a blender combine apricot halves,
tequila, sugar, lime juice, and apricot
nectar. Cover and blend until smooth.

With the blender running, gradually
add ice cubes, 1 cup at a time, through
opening in lid; blend until slushy. Pour
into prepared glasses to serve. If desired,
garnish with additional lime wedges.
Makes 8 (4-ounce) servings.

*FOR A NONALCOHOLIC BEVERAGE:
Prepare as above, except omit the tequila
and increase the apricot nectar to ¾ cup.

Crunchy Corn Snack Mix

*The lively spices in this munchable mix will
get everyone in the mood for what's to come.*

4 cups corn chips
3 cups bite-size corn or rice
    square cereal
2 cups bite-size cheese crackers
2 cups pretzel sticks
1½ cups mixed nuts
½ cup butter
2 tablespoons Worcestershire sauce
    for chicken
2 teaspoons chili powder
1 teaspoon garlic powder
1 teaspoon ground cumin

Preheat oven to 300°F. In a large
roasting pan combine corn chips, corn
cereal, cheese crackers, pretzels, and
nuts. Set aside.

In a small saucepan combine butter,
Worcestershire sauce, chili powder,
garlic powder, cumin, and if desired,
¼ teaspoon *cayenne pepper*; heat and stir
until butter melts. Drizzle butter mixture
over cereal mixture, stirring gently to coat.

Bake for 30 minutes, stirring every
10 minutes. Spread onto a large piece of
foil to cool. Store in an airtight container
for up to 2 weeks or freeze for up to
3 months. Makes 12 cups.

*Crunchy Corn
Snack Mix*

timetable for making it happen

Make the Double-Coconut Cream Pie and Crunchy Corn Snack Mix earlier in the day. That way you can have some savory munchies ready to welcome your guests and a dessert to end the party on a sweet note. Just before guests arrive, get out all the ingredients and utensils each team will need and separate them into workstations. If you have only one set of measuring cups and spoons, you may wish to ask a guest to lend you a set or two for the night to speed up the processes.

When friends arrive, divide them into four teams:

■ The Margarita and Entertainment Team: Ask people who'd rather not cook to whip up the Double Apricot Margaritas—in both spiked and unspiked versions. You also may want to offer a variety of beer and soft drinks. In addition, let them take charge of the game and music.

■ The Salad Team: Ask two friends to work on the Avocado and Apple Salad: One can slice the apples, avocado, and onions, while another can mix the dressing. Don't dress the salad until just before serving.

■ The Biscuit Team: This team of two takes care of the Cornmeal Pecan Biscuits. One cook can prepare the dough, while another toasts the pecans. While the biscuits bake, they can collaborate on the Chipotle-Orange Honey Butter.

■ The Stew Team: While you brown the meat for the Pork, Poblano, and Sweet Potato Stew, ask the two others on this team to peel, slice, chop, and measure the remaining ingredients.

What You'll Need...

- ☐ purchased plain white or natural canvas aprons
- ☐ acrylic paints in blue, gold, burgundy, and forest green, or to match the colors in the tray tiles
- ☐ acrylic textile medium
- ☐ heavy decorative paper or cardstock for the star
- ☐ bronze paper tack (available in scrapbooking stores and departments)

great cover-ups: painted aprons

1 Wash, dry, and iron the aprons as directed on the textile medium instructions. Mix the paints with textile medium according to the instructions. This helps the paint adhere to the fabric and makes it softer.

2 Enlarge the grid and star patterns on *page 155* to scale. Transfer the grid pattern to the apron and paint each square. When dry, set the paint as instructed on the textile medium instructions.

3 Cut the star from paper. Using the point of a scissors, make a hole through the star and apron and attach the star to the center of the grid with the tack. To launder the apron, remove the star.

What You'll Need...

- 17×17-inch purchased or self-made wooden tray
- sandpaper and tack cloth
- spray paint to match one tile color
- sixteen 4-inch-square ceramic tiles in gold, rust, brown, and forest green, or other desired colors
- tile adhesive
- spatula or small trowel
- grout
- sponge
- soft lint-free cloth

tile serving tray

1 Sand the tray and wipe it clean. Spray paint it with one or two coats of the desired color, sanding between coats.

2 On a flat surface, lay out the tiles in four rows, adjusting the colors to form a pleasant pattern.

3 Spread tile adhesive on the inside bottom of the tray following the manufacturer's directions. Transfer the tiles to the tray and press them in place. Leave an even space between each tile. Let the adhesive set.

4 Apply the grout according to the manufacturer's directions. Take care not to get grout onto the sides of the tray. After the grout dries, buff away any haze and polish the tile with a soft cloth.

Avocado and Apple Salad

Avocado and Apple Salad

This lime- and mint-sparked salad will provide a zippy, refreshing contrast to the more earthy and warm-spiced flavors of the Pork, Poblano, and Sweet Potato Stew.

⅓ cup olive oil
1 teaspoon finely shredded lime peel
2 tablespoons lime juice
2 tablespoons honey
1 tablespoon snipped fresh mint
½ teaspoon salt
12 cups torn romaine
2 green apples, cored and thinly sliced
2 avocados, halved, seeded, peeled, and sliced

1 small red onion, very thinly sliced and separated into rings
4 ounces queso fresco, ricotta salata, or farmer's cheese, crumbled (1 cup)
Freshly ground black pepper

In a screw-top jar combine olive oil, lime peel, lime juice, honey, mint, and salt. Cover and shake well. Set aside.

Place romaine onto a large serving platter. Top with apples, avocados, and onion. Shake dressing; drizzle over salad.

Sprinkle individual servings with cheese and pepper. Makes 8 servings.

star and quad invitations

1 Cut two 7×7½-inch rectangles from natural corrugated paper. Cut a 2-inch square from each of the other corrugated papers. Using foam dots, attach the small squares to the front of the invitation to form a grid. See the photograph, *above right*, for details. Note that the grid design is evenly spaced on the top, bottom, and right sides, and the left margin is larger to accommodate the tacks.

2 Enlarge the pattern on *page 155* and cut a star from decorative paper. Attach the star to the center of the grid using a tack.

3 If desired, scan the grid and star logo on *page 155*. Print the invitations with or without the logo. Cut out the invitation to fit the corrugated back.

4 Tape the invitation to the remaining piece of natural corrugated paper, centering it. Layer together the invitation front and back. Punch or poke holes for the tacks, spacing three tacks at equidistant points on the left side of the invitation. Insert the tacks to assemble the invitation.

Pork, Poblano, and
Sweet Potato Stew
Cornmeal Pecan Biscuits

84

Trim fat from pork. Cut pork into 1-inch cubes. In a 6- to 8-quart Dutch oven heat oil over medium-high heat. Cook pork, half at a time, in hot oil, turning to brown evenly. Remove pork.

Add onions, poblano peppers, sweet peppers, jalapeño peppers, and garlic to the Dutch oven. Cook over medium-high heat until onions are tender, stirring occasionally. Add broth, undrained tomatoes, lager, chili powder, cumin, oregano, salt, and black pepper. Add pork. Bring to boiling; reduce heat. Cover and simmer for 20 minutes.

Stir in sweet potatoes and black beans. Return to boiling; reduce heat. Cover and simmer about 20 minutes more or until meat and sweet potatoes are tender. To serve, ladle stew into bowls. If desired, garnish with cilantro sprigs. Makes 10 to 12 servings.

*NOTE: Because chile peppers contain volatile oils that can burn your skin and eyes, avoid direct contact with them as much as possible. When working with chile peppers, wear plastic or rubber gloves. If your bare hands do touch the peppers, wash your hands and nails well with soap and warm water.

Pork, Poblano, and Sweet Potato Stew

✳

If your crowd likes it hot, use more poblano peppers and fewer sweet peppers.

2½ pounds boneless pork
    shoulder roast
2 tablespoons olive oil
3 medium onions, halved and
    thickly sliced
2 medium fresh poblano chile
    peppers, seeded and cut into
    1-inch pieces*
2 medium red sweet peppers,
    seeded and cut into
    1-inch pieces

1 to 2 medium fresh jalapeño
    chile peppers, seeded and
    finely chopped*
6 cloves garlic, minced
2 14-ounce cans chicken broth
1 14½-ounce can diced tomatoes,
    undrained
½ cup lager or ale
1 teaspoon chili powder
1 teaspoon ground cumin
1 teaspoon dried oregano,
    crushed
½ teaspoon salt
¼ teaspoon black pepper
2 medium sweet potatoes (1 to
    1¼ pounds), peeled and
    coarsely chopped
1 15-ounce can black beans,
    rinsed and drained
    Fresh cilantro sprigs (optional)

Cornmeal Pecan Biscuits

The secret ingredient here is the cottage cheese—it brings unbelievable richness and creaminess to these luscious little biscuits.

1½ cups all-purpose flour
½ cup yellow cornmeal
2½ teaspoons baking powder
½ teaspoon salt
6 tablespoons butter
¾ cup small curd cream-style
    cottage cheese
⅔ cup milk
½ cup chopped pecans, toasted
1 recipe Chipotle-Orange
    Honey Butter

Preheat oven to 425°F. Line two baking sheets with parchment paper or foil; set aside.

In a large bowl stir together flour, cornmeal, baking powder, and salt. Using a pastry blender, cut in butter until mixture resembles coarse crumbs. Make a well in the center of flour mixture; set aside.

In a small bowl combine cottage cheese and milk; add all at once to flour mixture. Using a fork, stir just until moistened. Gently stir in pecans.

Drop dough into 16 mounds on prepared baking sheets (a scant ¼ cup dough per mound). Place baking sheets on separate oven racks. Bake for 14 to 16 minutes or until golden brown. Transfer to a wire rack. Serve warm biscuits with Chipotle-Orange Honey Butter. Makes 16 biscuits.

CHIPOTLE-ORANGE HONEY BUTTER: In a small bowl stir together ½ cup butter, softened; 2 tablespoons honey; 1 to 2 teaspoons finely chopped canned chipotle chile pepper in adobo sauce (see *Note on page 84); and 1 teaspoon finely shredded orange peel. Makes about ¾ cup butter.

85

What You'll Need...

- [ ] papier-mâché stars
- [ ] acrylic or spray paints to match the tile tray colors
- [ ] spray glitter
- [ ] several clusters of greenery

stars and greens centerpiece

1 Paint the stars with two or more coats of paint. Spray with glitter and set aside.

2 Purchase enough clusters of greenery to run down the center of the table. See the photograph *above* for details. Tuck the stem end of one cluster into the center of a second cluster, completely concealing it.

3 Working from the center out, continue in the same manner. The centerpiece should be narrower in the center, wider on the ends, and the greens should point outward from the center.

4 When the greens are arranged, tuck stars into them.

What You'll Need...

- purchased glass coasters designed for photo inserts
- vinegar
- clean, lint-free cloth
- glass paint in tomato red, burgundy, gold, sage, and blue or to match the tray tiles (see *page 158* for paint suggestions)
- 1 item of true trivia about each guest

What You'll Need...

- clear glass stemware and plain tumblers
- vinegar
- clean, lint-free cloth
- glass paint in gold, sage, blue, burgundy, and tomato red, or to match the tray tiles (see *page 158* for paint suggestions)

handpainted margarita glasses and tumblers

1. Thoroughly wash and dry the glassware. Wipe the surface with vinegar to remove any residue.

2. Using the photographs *below* and *opposite below* as a guide, paint the glassware in the desired geometric patterns. Read and follow the paint manufacturer's instructions before beginning to paint.

3. Follow the design lines of the glassware (stem, foot, bowl) for the basic colors, then add designs. Stripes can be drawn freehand or masked with narrow tape. Dots can be made with your finger, a pencil eraser, or the handle end of a brush. Let the base color dry completely before applying designs over it. Do not paint the upper 1 inch of the stemware near the rim.

4. Let the paint cure according to the manufacturer's instructions. NOTE: Some paints are cured by baking in the oven. These paints may be more durable and the cure time is shorter.

who's who game

1. Thoroughly clean the glass for each coaster, then wipe it with vinegar to remove any residue. Following the manufacturer's directions, paint each edge of the coasters a different color. See the photograph *above* for details.

2. Allow the paint to cure according to the manufacturer's directions.

3. Print out a coaster insert for each party guest. Include one piece of true trivia and two or more pieces of false trivia. See

the photograph *above* for details. Place the insert into the finished coaster.

4. To play the game, give every guest a coaster game piece. Let them find the person, then guess which piece of trivia is true and get details about that fact. When everyone sits down to dinner, the person holding that game coaster introduces the guest listed on his or her coaster and tells about the true trivia.

recipes to go

1 If desired, scan the logo on *page 155*. Type the recipes and print them with or without the logo onto good paper. See the photograph *above* for details.

2 Cut out the recipes and make a set for each guest to take home, as well as a set to use when cooking.

Double-Coconut Cream Pie

Prepare this opulent pie ahead of the party and have it waiting to reward your kitchen staff for a job well done.

3 egg whites
¼ cup cornstarch
¼ teaspoon salt
2 cups milk
¾ cup cream of coconut
3 beaten egg yolks
2 tablespoons butter

1 cup flaked coconut
2 teaspoons vanilla
½ teaspoon vanilla
¼ teaspoon cream of tartar
⅓ cup sugar
1 9-inch baked pastry shell, cooled*
2 tablespoons flaked coconut

Place egg whites in a large mixing bowl and let stand at room temperature for 30 minutes.

Meanwhile, for filling, in a medium saucepan combine cornstarch and salt; add ¼ cup of the milk, stirring until smooth. Stir in remaining 1¾ cups milk and the cream of coconut. Cook and stir over medium heat until thickened and bubbly. Cook and stir for 2 minutes more. Remove from heat. Gradually add about 1 cup of the hot filling to the egg yolks, stirring constantly. Pour egg yolk mixture into remaining hot filling in the saucepan. Bring to a gentle boil. Reduce heat; cook and stir for 2 minutes more.

Double-Coconut Cream Pie

Remove from heat. Stir in butter until melted. Stir in the 1 cup coconut and the 2 teaspoons vanilla. Keep warm.

Preheat oven to 350°F. For meringue, combine egg whites, the ½ teaspoon vanilla, and the cream of tartar. Beat with an electric mixer on medium speed about 1 minute or until soft peaks form (tips curl). Gradually add ⅓ cup sugar, 1 tablespoon at a time, beating on high speed about 4 minutes more or until mixture forms stiff peaks (tips stand straight) and sugar dissolves.

Spoon warm filling into cooled baked pastry shell. Immediately spread meringue over warm filling, carefully sealing to edge of the pastry to prevent shrinkage. Sprinkle with 2 tablespoons coconut. Bake for 15 minutes. Cool on wire rack for 1 hour. Chill for at least 3 hours or up to 6 hours before serving. Makes 8 servings.

*NOTE: For a 9-inch baked pastry shell, use your favorite pastry recipe, bake a 9-inch frozen unbaked deep-dish pastry shell according to package directions, or prepare and bake half of a 15-ounce package (1 crust) rolled refrigerated unbaked piecrust according to package directions.

87

chocolate for the

Bourbon-Chocolate Tipsy Cake

season

When it comes to sweets this season, you can't go wrong with chocolate. Here are eight recipes, each starring this all-time-favorite ingredient in irresistible ways, from sumptuous desserts and clever cookies to a great new take on hot chocolate.

Bourbon-Chocolate Tipsy Cake

Bourbon and coffee crystals add depth of flavor to this rich, super-moist cake. Whipped cream provides an airy contrast.

- 1 tablespoon unsweetened cocoa powder
- 2 cups all-purpose flour
- 1 teaspoon baking soda
- ½ teaspoon salt
- 3 ounces unsweetened chocolate, chopped
- 2 ounces sweet baking chocolate, chopped
- ¼ cup instant coffee crystals or instant espresso powder
- 2 tablespoons boiling water
- ½ cup bourbon
- 1 cup unsalted butter, softened
- 2 cups granulated sugar
- 3 eggs
- 1½ teaspoons vanilla
- 2 tablespoons bourbon
  Powdered sugar
  Fresh mint leaves (optional)
- 1 recipe Quick Sugared Cranberries (optional)

Preheat oven to 325°F. Butter a 10-inch fluted tube pan. Add cocoa powder to the pan. Shake and tilt pan to coat bottom, side, and tube with cocoa powder; shake out any excess cocoa powder. Set pan aside. In a medium bowl combine flour, baking soda, and salt; set aside.

In a small microwave-safe bowl combine unsweetened and sweet chocolates. Microwave, uncovered, on 100% power (high) for 1 minute; stir. Microwave for 30 seconds more. Stir until smooth. Set aside to cool slightly. In a 2-cup glass measure dissolve coffee crystals in the boiling water; add enough cold water to measure 1½ cups liquid. Stir in the ½ cup bourbon.

In a large mixing bowl beat butter with an electric mixer on medium to high speed for 30 seconds. Add granulated sugar; beat until well mixed. Beat in eggs, one at a time, beating well after each addition. Beat in melted chocolate and vanilla. Alternately add flour mixture and bourbon mixture to chocolate mixture, beginning and ending with flour mixture; beat on low speed after each addition just until combined. Pour into prepared pan.

Bake about 60 minutes or until a wooden toothpick inserted near the center of the cake comes out clean. Cool cake in pan on a wire rack for 15 minutes. Invert onto rack, remove pan, and cool completely. Brush top and side with the 2 tablespoons bourbon. (If desired, wrap in plastic wrap and store at room temperature for up to 2 days.)

To serve, sift powdered sugar over top of cake. If desired, garnish with fresh mint leaves and Quick Sugared Cranberries. Makes 12 to 16 servings.

QUICK SUGARED CRANBERRIES: Roll frozen cranberries in superfine sugar. As the cranberries begin to thaw, they will become coated with sugar.

Hot Caramel Chocolate
Milk Chocolate Mini Cookies

Milk Chocolate Mini Cookies

¾ cup all-purpose flour
¾ teaspoon baking powder
⅛ teaspoon salt
6 ounces milk chocolate pieces
3 tablespoons butter, softened
½ cup sugar
1 egg
¾ teaspoon vanilla
1 recipe Milk Chocolate-Sour Cream Frosting (optional)

In a medium bowl combine flour, baking powder, and salt; set aside.

In a small heavy saucepan heat chocolate over low heat until melted, stirring constantly. Set aside.

In a medium mixing bowl beat butter with an electric mixer on medium speed for 30 seconds. Beat in sugar until fluffy. Beat in melted chocolate, egg, and vanilla until combined.

Gradually beat in the flour mixture. Divide dough into four equal portions. Wrap each portion in plastic wrap. Chill in freezer for 20 to 30 minutes or until firm enough to handle. (Or chill in refrigerator for 1 hour.)

Preheat oven to 350°F. Line cookie sheets with parchment paper. Removing one portion of dough from freezer at a time, roll each portion into a log* about 10 inches long. Wrap and freeze for 5 minutes more. Cut each roll crosswise into ¼-inch-thick slices. Place slices 1 inch apart on prepared cookie sheets. Bake for 9 to 10 minutes or until edges are set. Let cool on cookie sheets for 2 minutes. Transfer cookies to a wire rack and let cool.

If desired, for sandwich cookies, spread Milk Chocolate-Sour Cream Frosting on half of the cookies, using ½ teaspoon of the frosting on each cookie; top with remaining cookies. Makes 144 tiny cookies or 72 tiny sandwich cookies.

MILK CHOCOLATE-SOUR CREAM FROSTING: In a medium saucepan combine 3 ounces milk chocolate pieces and 2 tablespoons butter; heat and stir over low heat until melted. Cool for 5 minutes. Stir in ¼ cup dairy sour cream. Gradually stir in 1 to 1¼ cups powdered sugar until spreadable.
*NOTE: Place dough on a sheet of waxed paper so you can use the paper to help shape the roll. If dough becomes too sticky, return to freezer for a few minutes.
TO STORE: Place unfilled cookies in layers separated by waxed paper in an airtight container; cover. Store at room temperature for up to 3 days. Or freeze in freezer container for up to 3 months. To serve, thaw cookies if frozen. If desired, fill with Milk Chocolate-Sour Cream Frosting just before serving.

Hot Caramel Chocolate

You'll be surprised at the lusciousness a little caramel adds to this favorite.

⅓ cup sugar
⅓ cup unsweetened cocoa powder
⅓ cup water
6 milk chocolate-covered round caramels (such as Rolo® candy)
6 cups half-and-half, light cream, or milk
Whipped cream (optional)
Unsweetened cocoa powder (optional)

In a large saucepan whisk together sugar and the ⅓ cup cocoa powder. Whisk in the water. Cook and stir over medium heat until sugar is dissolved. Add the caramels; cook and stir until melted. Stir in half-and-half; heat through, stirring occasionally. Pour into mugs. If desired, top with whipped cream and dust with unsweetened cocoa powder. Makes 6 (about 8-ounce) servings.

Chocolate Sherbet

Chocolate Sherbet

This chocolaty frozen treat makes the perfect light ending to a hearty holiday meal. Don't skimp on chilling time for the whipping cream mixture. It needs to be thoroughly chilled to freeze properly.

    6 to 7 ounces semisweet or
        bittersweet chocolate,
        chopped
    2 cups water
    ⅔ cup sugar
    ½ cup whipping cream
    1 teaspoon vanilla

In a medium saucepan stir together chopped chocolate, water, sugar, and whipping cream. Bring mixture to boiling, whisking constantly. Boil gently for 1 minute. Remove from heat; stir in vanilla. Cover and chill for 8 to 24 hours.

Freeze mixture in a 1-quart ice cream freezer according to manufacturer's directions. Ripen for 4 hours before serving.

To serve, scoop sherbet into small glasses or dishes. Makes 12 to 16 servings.

TEST KITCHEN TIP: Ripening homemade sherbet improves the texture and helps keep the sherbet from melting too quickly during eating.

To ripen the sherbet in a traditional-style ice cream freezer, after churning, remove the lid and dasher, and cover the top of the freezer can with waxed paper or foil. Plug the hole in the lid with a small piece of cloth; replace the lid. Pack the outer freezer bucket with enough ice and rock salt to cover the top of the freezer can (use 1 cup salt for each 4 cups ice). Ripen for 4 hours.

When using an ice cream freezer with an insulated freezer bowl, transfer the sherbet to a covered freezer container and ripen the sherbet by freezing it in your regular freezer for 4 hours (or check the ice cream freezer manufacturer's recommendations).

Chocolate-Raspberry Yule Log

Chocolate-Raspberry
Yule Log

✳

Carry on the tradition of garnishing a cake roll to look like a yule log. When preparing the cake, the pan you use needs to be 1 inch deep to hold the batter.

⅔ cup all-purpose flour
⅓ cup unsweetened cocoa powder
¼ teaspoon salt
5 egg yolks
2 tablespoons milk
1 teaspoon vanilla
1 cup granulated sugar
5 egg whites
¼ teaspoon cream of tartar
  Powdered sugar
1 tablespoon raspberry liqueur
  (optional)
⅓ cup seedless raspberry jam
1 quart French vanilla ice cream
1 recipe Chocolate Ganache
  Fresh raspberries (optional)
  Fresh bay leaves (optional)

Preheat oven to 375°F. Grease and lightly flour a 15×10×1-inch jelly roll pan; set aside. In a small bowl stir together flour, cocoa powder, and salt; set aside.

In a medium mixing bowl beat egg yolks, milk, and vanilla with an electric mixer on high speed for 4 to 5 minutes or until thick and lemon colored. Gradually add ½ cup of the granulated sugar; beat on high speed until sugar is dissolved.

Thoroughly wash beaters. In a large mixing bowl beat egg whites and cream of tartar with electric mixer on medium to high speed until soft peaks form (tips curl). Gradually add the remaining ½ cup granulated sugar, 2 tablespoons at a time, beating until stiff peaks form (tips stand straight). Fold 1 cup of the egg white mixture into the egg yolk mixture. Fold egg yolk mixture into remaining egg white mixture. Fold in flour mixture. Spread batter evenly in prepared pan.

Bake for 12 to 15 minutes or until cake springs back when lightly touched. Immediately loosen edges of cake from pan and turn cake out onto a clean kitchen towel sprinkled with powdered sugar. Starting from one of the cake's short sides, roll up towel and warm cake into a spiral. Cool on a wire rack.

Unroll cake onto a large baking sheet. Don't worry if cake cracks; just unroll and roll carefully. Cracks will be covered by the ganache. If desired, stir raspberry liqueur into the jam. Spread half of the jam on the cake. In a chilled large bowl stir ice cream with a wooden spoon just until softened enough to spread. Spread ice cream over jam to within 1 inch of the edges and ends. Drizzle or dab remaining jam over ice cream. If necessary for easier rolling, place baking sheet with cake in the freezer for 15 minutes or just until ice cream is firm. Roll up cake without towel, using towel to lift cake as you roll. Cover with plastic wrap. Freeze for 4 hours or up to 1 week.

When ready to serve, spoon Chocolate Ganache over log and spread with a spatula to create bark texture. Freeze up to 30 minutes before serving. If desired, garnish log with raspberries and fresh bay leaves. Makes 10 servings.

CHOCOLATE GANACHE: In a small saucepan bring ½ cup whipping cream to boiling over medium-high heat. Remove from heat. Add 6 ounces semisweet or bittersweet chocolate, chopped (do not stir). Let stand for 5 minutes. Stir until smooth. Let cool about 45 to 60 minutes before using. Ganache should thicken enough to be of spreading consistency.

Bittersweet Mousse

Chocolate has an affinity to many fruits, but poached pears may rank as one of its most elegant partners. Conveniently, pears are in season around the holidays.

    1½ cups whipping cream
     8 ounces bittersweet or semisweet
          chocolate, coarsely chopped
     2 beaten egg yolks
    ⅓ cup sugar
    ¼ cup water
     1 recipe Spiced Poached Pears
          (see recipe, right)
          Chocolate shavings or whipped
          cream (optional)

In a small heavy saucepan combine ½ cup of the whipping cream, chopped chocolate, egg yolks, sugar, and water. Cook and stir over medium heat just until mixture starts to bubble around edges. Remove from heat. Pour mixture into a large bowl which has been set in a bowl of ice water. Cool for 15 to 20 minutes, stirring frequently.

Pour the remaining 1 cup whipping cream into a chilled medium mixing bowl. Beat with the chilled beaters of an

Bittersweet Mousse with Spiced Poached Pears

electric mixture on medium speed just until thickened (do not beat to soft peaks or finished mousse will be too stiff). Fold into cooled chocolate mixture. Cover and chill for 2 to 24 hours.

Spoon mousse into individual dessert bowls. Serve with Spiced Poached Pears. If desired, top with chocolate shavings or whipped cream. Makes 8 servings.

Spiced Poached Pears

This recipe was designed to partner perfectly with the Bittersweet Mousse.

     4 medium pears (about 2 pounds)
     1 750-ml bottle dry white wine
          or 3 cups apple juice or
          apple cider
     2 cups water
     1 cup sugar
     3 inches stick cinnamon, broken
     1 2-inch-long piece peeled fresh
          ginger, cut into strips

Peel pears, leaving stems intact. Cut each pear in half. Use a melon baller to remove the core.

Meanwhile, in a 4-quart Dutch oven combine wine, water, sugar, cinnamon, and ginger. Cook, uncovered, over medium heat until gently boiling, stirring occasionally to dissolve sugar. Add pears. Return liquid just to boiling; reduce heat. Cover and simmer for 25 to 30 minutes or just until pears are tender.

Remove from heat; cool pears slightly in syrup. Transfer to a very large bowl. Cover and chill for 2 to 24 hours. Drain pears to serve. Makes 8 servings.

Chocolate Tartlets

Chocolate Tartlets

Every bite is a chocolaty extravaganza! Bake these treats for your favorite chocolate lover this holiday season.

⅔ cup whipping cream
3 ounces semisweet or bittersweet chocolate, chopped
3 ounces milk chocolate, chopped
1 recipe Cream Cheese Tart Shells Powdered sugar (optional)

For filling, in a small saucepan heat whipping cream over medium heat just to simmering. Remove from heat. Place semisweet chocolate and milk chocolate in a medium mixing bowl; pour hot cream over chocolate. Let stand for 5 minutes (do not stir). Stir until chocolate is melted and smooth. Cover and chill for 1 hour.

Beat chilled chocolate mixture with an electric mixer on medium speed just until soft peaks form (tips curl). Spoon or pipe mixture into cooled Cream Cheese Tart Shells. Cover and chill for 2 hours or up to 3 days.

If desired, sprinkle tartlets with powdered sugar just before serving. Makes 24 tartlets.

CREAM CHEESE TART SHELLS: Preheat oven to 325°F. In a medium bowl combine ½ cup butter, softened, and one 3-ounce package cream cheese, softened. Beat with an electric mixer until smooth. Stir in 1 cup all-purpose flour. If necessary, cover and chill dough about 30 minutes or until easy to handle. Press a slightly rounded teaspoon of the dough evenly onto the bottom and up the side of each of 24 ungreased 1¾-inch muffin cups. Bake for 25 to 30 minutes or until pastry is golden brown on edges. Cool in pans on wire racks for 5 minutes. Carefully remove tart shells from pans. Cool completely on wire racks.

chocolate tips and tricks

Get the most out of your chocolate recipes by keeping these hints in mind.

■ Real chocolate is made with cocoa butter, chocolate liquor (the pressed liquid from roasted cocoa beans), and sugar. When a recipe calls for chocolate, be sure to use the real product. Imitations substitute vegetable fat for the cocoa butter, and the difference in taste is obvious.

■ Semisweet and bittersweet chocolate can be used interchangeably in cooking.

■ Store chocolate well wrapped in a cool (55°F to 65°F) place; it will keep up to 1 year.

■ If the chocolate develops a grayish haze on its surface, don't throw it away. This gray color (known as bloom) may look unappetizing, but it disappears when heated and will not affect the outcome of your recipes. The bloom appears when chocolate is stored in conditions that are too humid or warm.

■ When melting chocolate, be sure there are no water drops in the pan or on any of the utensils you're using. Also avoid letting water splatter into the chocolate as it melts. Even a few drops of water can cause the melting chocolate to "seize," or develop an undesired grainy texture.

Pistachio Brownie Wedges

Pistachio Brownie Wedges

Chocolate-drizzled and nut-sprinkled wedges bring a new shape to the holiday cookie plate.

½ cup butter
3 ounces unsweetened chocolate
2 eggs
¾ cup sugar
1 teaspoon vanilla
¾ cup all-purpose flour
¾ cup coarsely chopped pistachio nuts
1 ounce white baking chocolate (with cocoa butter), chopped

Preheat oven to 325°F. Line the bottom of a 9x1½-inch round baking pan with waxed paper; grease waxed paper and side of pan. Set aside.

In a small saucepan combine butter and unsweetened chocolate. Heat and stir over low heat until melted and smooth. Remove from heat; let stand at room temperature until cool.

In a large mixing bowl beat eggs with an electric mixer on high speed about 1 minute or until frothy. Add sugar and vanilla; beat about 2 minutes or until thick and lemon colored. Beat in melted unsweetened chocolate mixture. Stir in flour. Spread into prepared baking pan.

Sprinkle evenly with pistachio nuts; press lightly into batter.

Bake for 25 minutes. Cool in pan on a wire rack. Remove from pan. Remove waxed paper.

Place white baking chocolate in a small microwave-safe bowl. Microwave on 70% power (medium-high) for 1 minute; stir until melted and smooth. Drizzle over brownies and let stand until set. Cut brownie into quarters; cut each quarter into 4 wedges. Makes 16 wedges.

TO STORE: Place wedges in a single layer in a freezer container; cover. Freeze for up to 1 month.

Apple-Lemon Sparkler
Baked Fennel Blue Cheese Dip

hot dips, cool drinks

Sure, you could fuss over all kinds of intricate little appetizer nibbles, but the easy and oozy hot cheese dips will disappear first. Here are four great takes, alongside five frosty and festive drinks. Mix and match them for an irresistible way to jump-start any holiday gathering.

Apple-Lemon Sparkler

Sometimes people who don't drink alcohol have to settle for the same old soda selection. Serve this tangy and fizzy sipper to let nondrinkers toast the season in style.

　8　cups apple juice or apple cider, chilled
　½　of a 12-ounce can (¾ cup) frozen lemonade concentrate, thawed
　1　1-liter bottle carbonated water, chilled
　　　Ice cubes
　9　lady apples, halved (optional)

In a punch bowl stir together apple juice and thawed lemonade concentrate. Slowly pour chilled carbonated water

down side of bowl; stir gently to mix. Serve over ice. If desired, garnish individual servings with apple halves. Makes 18 (6-ounce) servings.

Baked Fennel Blue Cheese Dip

The licorice-like tones of fennel combine with blue cheese and bacon for one unbelievably good party dip.

　4　slices bacon
　3　medium fennel bulbs* (8 ounces each)
　2　cloves garlic, minced
　1　8-ounce jar mayonnaise
　1　8-ounce carton dairy sour cream
　1　4-ounce package crumbled blue cheese
　20　dried whole black or pink peppercorns, crushed
　2　tablespoons finely shredded Parmesan cheese
　2　tablespoons fine dry bread crumbs
　　　Toasted baguette-style French bread slices and/or assorted vegetable dippers, such as jicama sticks, Belgian endive leaves, and/or baby carrots

Preheat oven to 400°F. In a large skillet cook bacon over medium heat until crisp. Remove bacon and drain on paper towels,

reserving 1 tablespoon drippings in skillet. Crumble bacon and set aside.

To prepare fennel, cut off and discard upper stalks of fennel. Remove any wilted outer layers and cut a thin slice from the fennel base. Wash fennel and cut in half lengthwise; remove core. Cut crosswise into very thin slices.

Add fennel and garlic to reserved drippings in skillet. Cook over medium heat about 10 minutes or just until fennel is tender and begins to brown, stirring occasionally. Remove from heat. Add crumbled bacon, mayonnaise, sour cream, blue cheese, and peppercorns to fennel; mix well. Divide mixture between two 16-ounce ovenproof crocks, soufflé dishes, or other ovenproof dishes.

In a small bowl combine Parmesan cheese and bread crumbs; sprinkle over mixture in crocks.

Bake, uncovered, about 15 minutes or just until mixture is heated through and tops are light brown. Do not overbake. Serve with toasted bread slices and/or vegetable dippers. Makes 8 to 10 (about ½-cup) servings.

*****NOTE:** If you prefer, substitute 4½ cups shredded cabbage or 3½ cups chopped cauliflower for the fennel. Cook as directed.

Sparkling Cranberry Rosé

Be sure to choose a dry rosé (not a white Zinfandel) for this recipe; a good choice would be one from the Rhône or Languedoc region of France.

- 1¼ cups cranberry juice, chilled
- 1 750-ml bottle sparkling extra-dry rosé wine, champagne, or sparkling white grape juice, chilled
- 10 sugar cubes
  Fresh cranberries (optional)

Pour cranberry juice into a small punch bowl. Slowly pour the chilled wine, champagne, or grape juice down the side of the bowl; stir gently to mix.
To serve, place a sugar cube in the bottom of each of 10 chilled tall, narrow glasses. Carefully ladle punch mixture into each glass. If desired, garnish with skewered fresh cranberries. Makes 10 (about 4-ounce) servings.

Orange Martinis

Have a pitcher of the vodka or gin mixture ready and waiting in the fridge, then shake up the martinis ice cold as guests arrive.

- Orange wedge
- Sugar
- 3 cups vodka or gin
- 6 tablespoons frozen orange juice concentrate, thawed
- ⅓ cup dry vermouth
- Ice cubes
- Orange peel twists (optional)

Rub orange wedge around the rims of 11 martini glasses. Invert glasses into a dish of sugar to coat rims. Shake off any excess sugar. Set aside.
In a small pitcher combine vodka, orange juice concentrate, and vermouth.

Place ice cubes in a martini shaker. For each drink, add ⅓ cup of the vodka mixture; shake. Strain into one of the prepared martini glasses. If desired, garnish individual servings with an orange peel twist. Makes 11 (about 3-ounce) servings.
APPLE MARTINIS: Prepare as directed, except substitute ¾ cup frozen apple juice concentrate, thawed, for the thawed orange juice concentrate. If desired, garnish with orange peel twists. Makes 12 (about 3-ounce) servings.

Crab and Horseradish Havarti Dip

Horseradish and chive Havarti cheese lets you add a windfall of flavors with just one ingredient. If you can't find it, see the note below for an easy substitution.

- 1 8-ounce package cream cheese, softened
- 1¼ cups shredded horseradish and chive Havarti cheese* (5 ounces)
- ⅓ cup dairy sour cream
- ¼ cup mayonnaise
- 1 cup cooked crabmeat or one 6-ounce can crabmeat, drained, flaked, and cartilage removed
- 1 cup shredded fresh baby spinach
- ⅓ cup thinly sliced green onions
  Flatbread, bagel chips, crostini, and/or toasted baguette-style French bread slices

Preheat oven to 350°F. In a large mixing bowl combine cream cheese, 1 cup of the Havarti cheese, the sour cream, and mayonnaise; beat with an electric mixer on medium speed until well mixed. Gently stir in crabmeat and spinach.
Transfer mixture to a 1-quart baking dish. Bake, uncovered, about 25 minutes or until bubbly and heated through. Sprinkle with the remaining ¼ cup Havarti cheese and

new American cheeses

These days, more and more American states are home to cheese makers who produce their own unique handcrafted treasures that rival the famous cheeses of Europe. Seek them out at specialty cheese shops or in well-stocked supermarkets. Serve them simply with crackers, bread, and/or fruit, or try them in the recipes on these pages. Here are a few examples:

■ Vermont Cheddar Cheeses: Handcrafted Vermont cheddar cheeses are richer, creamier, and have fuller flavor than the usual commercial varieties. Two high-quality, highly regarded cheeses are Cabot Creamery Cheddar and Shelburne Farms Cheddar. You'll notice that many handcrafted versions of cheddar cheese are white in color rather than orange. That's because they lack a natural dye called annatto, which gives the orange varieties their color.

■ Point Reyes Original Blue: This classic-style blue cow's milk cheese is handcrafted on a family dairy farm in Point Reyes, California. The creamy, full-flavored cheese has garnered rave reviews since it appeared in 2000. Try it with a glass of port and an array of hazelnuts and walnuts for an after-dinner, into-the-evening indulgence.

■ Roth Käse Ostenborg Horseradish and Chive Havarti: The Crab and Horseradish Havarti Dip, *left,* is a terrific way to showcase this robust cheese from Wisconsin. Another time, substitute it for Swiss to perk up a Reuben sandwich. Or serve it sliced at room temperature with party rye bread.

the green onions. Serve with assorted breads. Makes 12 (¼-cup) servings.
***NOTE:** If you can't find the horseradish and chive Havarti cheese, substitute 1¼ cups shredded Havarti and add 1 tablespoon snipped fresh chives and 2 teaspoons prepared horseradish with the sour cream.

Sparkling Cranberry Rosé
Orange Martinis
Crab and Horseradish Havarti Dip

Fruit Cooler
Fontina Cheese and Three-Onion Gratin

Fontina Cheese and Three-Onion Gratin

Members of the onion family (sweet onions, leeks, and shallots) team up with two great cheeses (fontina and Asiago) for another dip that will disappear fast.

- 2 tablespoons butter or margarine
- 1 large sweet onion, such as Vidalia, Maui, or Walla Walla, chopped (2 cups)
- 2 leeks, thinly sliced
- ⅓ cup finely chopped shallots
- 2 cloves garlic, minced
- 1 8-ounce package cream cheese, cubed
- 6 ounces fontina cheese, shredded (1½ cups)
- 2 ounces Asiago cheese, finely shredded (½ cup)
- 1 tablespoon snipped assorted fresh herbs, such as basil, sage, flat-leaf parsley, and/or thyme (optional)
  Bagel chips, crackers, and/or toasted baguette-style French bread slices

Preheat oven to 350°F. In a large skillet melt butter over medium heat. Add onion, leeks, shallots, and garlic; cook for 5 to 10 minutes or until onion is tender and lightly browned, stirring frequently (watch closely to prevent overbrowning). Remove from heat. Stir in cream cheese, fontina cheese, and Asiago cheese; let stand for 2 minutes to soften. Stir until well mixed.

Transfer mixture to a 1- to 1½-quart baking dish. Bake, uncovered, about 15 minutes or until bubbly and hot. If desired, sprinkle with herbs. Serve with bagel chips, crackers, and/or toasted bread slices. Makes 8 (¼-cup) servings.

Fruit Cooler

Anything that calls for nectar—the drink of the gods—has to be good. Your friends who prefer a nonalcoholic choice will love this delicious drink, too.

1½ cups peach nectar, chilled
½ cup orange juice, chilled
¼ cup unsweetened grapefruit juice, chilled
1 tablespoon lemon juice
Ice cubes
1½ cups sparkling mineral water, chilled
Kiwifruit slices (optional)

In a pitcher stir together peach nectar, orange juice, grapefruit juice, and lemon juice. Divide mixture among four 10-ounce glasses filled with ice. Top individual servings with mineral water. If desired, garnish with kiwifruit slices. Makes 4 (about 8-ounce) servings.

*Frosty Raspberry Margaritas
Warm Artichoke and Salsa Dip*

Warm Artichoke and Salsa Dip

Update the ever-popular artichoke dip with a Tex-Mex twist using salsa, Monterey Jack cheese, and cilantro.

1 12-ounce jar or two 6-ounce jars marinated artichoke hearts
⅓ cup sliced green onions
2 tablespoons bottled green salsa
½ cup shredded Monterey Jack or white cheddar cheese (2 ounces)
¼ cup dairy sour cream
¼ cup snipped fresh cilantro
Assorted vegetable dippers, such as carrot slices, celery sticks, or sweet pepper strips; crackers; and/or toasted baguette-style French bread slices

Drain artichokes; coarsely chop. In a small saucepan combine chopped artichokes, green onions, and salsa. Cook over medium heat until heated through, stirring frequently. Remove from heat. Stir in cheese, sour cream, and cilantro. Serve immediately with vegetable dippers, crackers, and/or toasted bread slices. Makes 6 (¼-cup) servings.

Frosty Raspberry Margaritas

Frozen fruit-juice concentrate provides a convenient base for these cool and fruity cocktails.

Lime wedge
Sugar
¾ cup tequila
½ cup frozen raspberry juice blend concentrate, thawed
⅓ cup raspberry liqueur
¼ cup Triple Sec or other orange liqueur
¼ cup lime juice
5 cups ice cubes
Fresh raspberries (optional)
Lime peel twists (optional)

Rub lime wedge around the rims of seven frozen margarita glasses or 8-ounce glasses. Invert glasses into a dish of sugar to coat rims. Shake off any excess sugar. Set aside.

In a blender combine tequila, juice blend concentrate, raspberry liqueur, Triple Sec, and lime juice. Cover and blend until well mixed.

With the blender running, gradually add ice cubes, 1 cup at a time, through opening in lid; blend until slushy.

Pour blended mixture into prepared glasses. If desired, garnish with fresh raspberries and lime peel twists. Makes 7 (about 8-ounce) servings.

Spinach Salad with Leeks and Pancetta

This New Year's Eve, use a menu of classic French flavors and some clever decorating ideas to transport guests to a bustling Parisian bistro without leaving your home.

bistro
magnifique

The original French bistros were simply wine merchants' shops that eventually evolved into humble restaurants that served wine with their homey food. These days on either side of the Atlantic, a bistro can be cozy and small or large and bustling, but all share the warm, personable appeal of their forbearers. There are no vast dining rooms with huge chandeliers, no formally tuxedoed maître d's. At a bistro an atmosphere of coziness and intimacy abounds.

Uncomplicated cooking—such as rustic roasts and hearty stews—is the specialty of the traditional French bistro kitchen. Trendy bistros often offer such classics alongside dishes wrought with inventive touches.

To mimic the intimacy of a tiny French bistro in your own home, set up multiple small dining tables instead of one large one. A black-and-white color scheme, crisp white linens, and geometric patterns emphasize the cafe feel, while Parisian souvenirs lend a touch of romance.

Spinach Salad with Leeks and Pancetta

After years of starring on menus in French bistros, poached egg salads are making a splash in American restaurants.

- 6 ounces thick-slice pancetta (9 slices) or bacon (5 slices)
- 2 tablespoons olive oil
  Cooking oil or shortening
- 8 eggs
- 2 small leeks (white part only), thinly sliced
- ⅓ cup white wine vinegar or white vinegar
- 1 teaspoon sugar
- 12 cups fresh baby spinach or regular spinach leaves (9- to 10-ounce package)
- ½ cup finely shredded Parmesan cheese (2 ounces)
  Freshly ground black pepper

In a large skillet cook pancetta or bacon over medium-high heat until crisp. Remove pancetta or bacon from skillet, reserving 2 tablespoons drippings in skillet. Drain pancetta or bacon on paper towels. Crumble and set aside. Add the olive oil to drippings in skillet; set aside.

Lightly grease another very large skillet with cooking oil or shortening. Add water to half-fill the skillet. Bring water to boiling; reduce heat to simmering (bubbles should begin to break surface). Break one of the eggs into a measuring cup. Carefully slide egg into simmering water, holding the lip of the cup as close to the water as possible. Repeat with remaining eggs, allowing each egg an equal amount of space.

Simmer eggs, uncovered, for 3 to 5 minutes or until whites are completely set and yolks begin to thicken but are not hard. Using a slotted spoon, remove eggs from skillet to paper towels. If desired, trim edges with a knife.

Meanwhile, for dressing, add leeks to reserved drippings and olive oil in skillet; cook and stir just until tender. Add vinegar and sugar to the skillet. Bring to boiling; reduce heat. Simmer, uncovered, for 2 minutes.

In a very large bowl* combine spinach, crumbled pancetta or bacon, and hot dressing; toss to coat. Divide salad among eight salad plates. Top each salad with a poached egg. Sprinkle with Parmesan and pepper. Makes 8 servings.

MAKE-AHEAD TIP: To cut down on some of the last-minute preparation, poach the eggs ahead and hold them in a bowl of warm water for up to 20 minutes.

***NOTE:** If your bowl won't hold all of the spinach, start by tossing 8 cups of spinach with the pancetta or bacon and dressing until it starts to wilt. Then add remaining spinach and toss again.

fragrant welcome

A lavender-covered wreath greets everyone with the soft scent of Provence. That familiar French icon, the *Tour Eiffel*, is framed by the rectangular wreath.

1 Brush one section of a 12×7-inch rectangular green plastic foam wreath form with tacky crafts glue. NOTE: If a green wreath form is not available, paint a form green with spray paint appropriate for plastic foam. Press the lavender buds into the wet glue. Repeat until the entire wreath is covered in lavender buds. After the glue dries, hot-glue stems of lavender to the face of the wreath. Work around the wreath laying bundles of lavender in place as shown *above*, making sure all stem ends of one bundle are covered by the buds of the next bundle.

2 Wrap wide white satin ribbon around the wreath at the center of each side. Pin it in place on the back of the wreath. Center narrower checked ribbon over the white ribbon and pin it in place. Use narrow ribbon to hang an Eiffel Tower ornament in the center of the wreath.

Roasted Lamb with Olive Tapenade
Thyme-Roasted Beets
Root Vegetable Mash, page 105
Mushroom Medley, page 107

Roasted Lamb with Olive Tapenade

Gigot d'agneau—leg of lamb—is a quintessential bistro dish. This recipe imbues it with typical Provençal touches, including garlic, herbs, and olives.

- 1 cup pitted kalamata olives
- 1 tablespoon snipped fresh flat-leaf parsley
- 1 tablespoon olive oil
- 1 teaspoon finely shredded lemon peel
- 2 teaspoons lemon juice
- 1 teaspoon snipped fresh rosemary
- 1 teaspoon snipped fresh thyme
- ¼ teaspoon freshly ground black pepper
- 2 cloves garlic, minced
- 1 3½- to 4-pound boneless leg of lamb, rolled and tied
- ⅓ cup dry red wine
- 1 teaspoon kosher salt
- 1 teaspoon freshly ground black pepper

For olive tapenade, in a food processor combine olives, parsley, oil, lemon peel, lemon juice, rosemary,

thyme, the ¼ teaspoon pepper, and garlic. Cover and process until finely chopped, stopping to scrape down sides as necessary. Set aside.

Preheat oven to 325°F. Untie and unroll roast. Trim fat. If necessary, place meat, boned side up, between two pieces of plastic wrap and pound meat with a meat mallet to an even thickness. Spread olive mixture over cut surface of meat. Roll up; tie securely with 100-percent cotton kitchen string.

Place roast, seam side down, on a rack in a shallow roasting pan. In a small bowl combine wine, salt, and the 1 teaspoon pepper. Roast for 1¾ to 2¼ hours or until an instant-read thermometer inserted into the center of the roast registers 140°F for medium-rare doneness; baste with wine mixture several times until the last 10 minutes of roasting. Discard any remaining wine mixture.

Remove roast from oven. Cover with foil and let stand for 15 minutes before slicing. Temperature of the meat after standing should be 150°F. Remove strings and slice meat. Makes 8 servings.

Thyme-Roasted Beets

French chefs really know how to cook beets. Often they roast them, bringing out their mellow, sweet flavors. Here we drizzled them with a lemon-herb mixture for an up-to-date touch.

- 3½ to 4 pounds baby beets (assorted colors) or small beets
- 6 cloves garlic
- 3 sprigs fresh thyme
- 5 tablespoons olive oil
- ½ teaspoon kosher salt
- ¼ teaspoon freshly ground black pepper
- 2 tablespoons lemon juice
- 1 tablespoon snipped fresh thyme Snipped fresh thyme (optional)

Preheat oven to 400°F. Cut tops off the beets and trim the root ends. Wash beets thoroughly. If using small beets, cut into 1- to 1½-inch wedges. Place beets into a 3-quart rectangular baking dish. Add garlic and thyme sprigs. In a small bowl stir together 3 tablespoons of the olive oil, salt, and pepper. Drizzle over vegetables in dish; toss lightly to coat. Cover dish with foil.

Roast for 40 to 45 minutes or until tender. (A knife should slide easily into the beets when they are tender.) Uncover and let beets cool in pan on a wire rack about 15 minutes. If using small beets, remove skins by wrapping the wedges, one at a time, in a paper towel and gently rubbing off the skins (use new paper towels as needed). Baby beets do not need to be peeled.

Remove garlic from dish and finely chop. Discard thyme sprigs. In a small bowl combine garlic, the remaining 2 tablespoons olive oil, lemon juice, and the 1 tablespoon snipped thyme. Drizzle mixture over beets; toss lightly to coat.

To serve, if desired, sprinkle individual servings with additional snipped thyme. Serve warm or at room temperature. Makes 8 servings.

105

Root Vegetable Mash

In recent years, American bistros have steered mashed potatoes into gourmet territory. This recipe follows that lead, but it uses other root vegetables for delightfully different flavors.

 1 large rutabaga (about
    1¾ pounds), peeled and cut
    into 1-inch pieces
1½ pounds turnips, peeled and cut
    into 2-inch pieces
1½ pounds parsnips, peeled and cut
    into 2-inch pieces
 6 cloves garlic, peeled
 2 tablespoons butter
 ¼ to ⅓ cup half-and-half or
    light cream
    Kosher salt
    Freshly ground black pepper

In a covered large saucepan cook rutabaga, turnips, parsnips, and garlic in enough boiling salted water to cover for 30 to 35 minutes or until vegetables are tender. Drain.

Mash the vegetable mixture with a potato masher (mixture should be coarsely mashed with some vegetable pieces remaining). Stir in butter and enough of the half-and-half to make desired consistency. Season to taste with salt and pepper. Makes 8 servings.

neighborhood bistro

Set up your own bistro using small tables. Placing them close together encourages conversation between tables, much like what happens between diners in a true bistro. Metal tables and chairs reminiscent of sidewalk cafes were used here, but folding tables or inexpensive round wooden knockdown tables from the discount store would work as well.

*Prosciutto-and-Basil-
Stuffed Turkey Breast*

Prosciutto-and-Basil-Stuffed Turkey Breast

*Though prosciutto is a quintessential
Italian ingredient, the French enjoy it too.
They call it "jambon de Parme"—Parma
ham, which refers to Parma, Italy, a city
known for its superior prosciutto. The
turkey can be an alternate to the lamb.*

  2 3- to 3½-pound fresh or frozen
      bone-in turkey breast halves
      Nonstick cooking spray
  4 ounces thinly sliced prosciutto
 12 small or 6 large fresh basil leaves
  ½ cup butter, melted
  ¼ cup finely chopped shallots
  2 cloves garlic, minced
  1 14-ounce can chicken broth
  ¼ cup all-purpose flour
  2 tablespoons snipped fresh basil

Thaw turkey, if frozen. Preheat oven
to 400°F. Coat a large shallow roasting
pan and rack with nonstick cooking spray.
Place turkey breast halves, bone sides
down, on roasting rack in prepared pan.
Starting at breast bone of each
breast half, slip your fingers between
skin and meat to loosen the skin, leaving
skin attached at top. Lift skin and
arrange prosciutto slices and basil leaves
over breast meat. Insert an oven-going
meat thermometer into the thickest part
of one of the turkey breasts, being sure
bulb does not touch bone.

Roast, uncovered, on lower rack of oven
for 20 minutes. Meanwhile, in a small
bowl stir together melted butter, shallots,
garlic, ½ teaspoon *salt,* and ¼ teaspoon
freshly ground *black pepper.* Reduce oven
temperature to 350°F. Roast for 1 to
1½ hours more or until thermometer

registers 170°F, juices run clear, and
turkey is no longer pink, occasionally
spooning butter mixture over turkey
breasts. Let stand, covered with foil, for
10 minutes before slicing.

Meanwhile, pour pan drippings into
a 2-cup glass measure, scraping up
browned bits. Skim off fat; pour ¼ cup of
the fat into a medium saucepan. Discard
remaining fat. Add enough broth to the
drippings in the measuring cup to equal
2 cups total liquid.

Stir flour into fat in saucepan. Stir
drippings mixture into flour mixture in
saucepan. Stir in snipped basil. Cook and
stir over medium heat until thickened and
bubbly. Cook and stir for 1 minute more.
Season to taste with additional salt and
freshly ground black pepper. Serve gravy
with sliced turkey. Makes 8 servings.

Mushroom Medley

Ever notice how today's bistros often stack foods for a dramatic effect? Tap into the trend by topping Root Vegetable Mash (recipe, page 105) with this mixture.

    4 ounces fresh chanterelle
       mushrooms or 2 ounces dried
       chanterelle mushrooms
   12 ounces assorted fresh
       mushrooms, such as cremini,
       button, shiitake, and/or oyster
    ¼ cup butter
    3 cloves garlic, minced
    2 tablespoons snipped fresh
       flat-leaf parsley
    ½ teaspoon kosher salt
       Freshly ground black pepper

Clean all fresh mushrooms and trim stem ends. (If using dried chanterelle mushrooms, place in a bowl; add just enough boiling water to cover. Let dried mushrooms stand for 15 minutes. Drain, rinse, and drain mushrooms again. Remove stems and discard.) Slice any large mushrooms.

In a large skillet heat butter over medium-high heat until melted. Add garlic; cook and stir for 30 seconds. Add mushrooms. Cook and stir about 5 minutes or just until tender. Remove from heat. Stir in parsley and salt. Season to taste with pepper. Makes 8 servings.

ribbon-striped linens

🌿 Using iron-on fusible web tape or fabric glue, embellish plain white dinner napkins and tablecloths with a border of ⅞-inch-wide black satin ribbon. Place the ribbon about 1 inch in from the outer edge. The hem stitching often falls at this point and can be used as a guide. The ribbon also can be edgestitched to the linens for a more permanent treatment.

Use the ribbon-striped napkins as chair backs by draping them diagonally over the chair back and adding framed artwork. For the dinner napkins, omit the ribbon trim.

great backup

🌿 Soften the look of each chair with an easy chair back cover. Trim white dinner napkins with black satin ribbon as described *above*.

Eyelets placed in opposing corners allow the napkins to be joined at the bottom by a black frame. A small piece of art, some decorative paper, or a trinket is suspended within each frame. See *page 108* for details on the Chair Frames.

art smart

🌿 When thinking of France, art and architecture come to mind. Incorporate both in your dining decor by using framed art tied on a ribbon for the napkin ring.

Spray paint miniature frames from the scrapbooking department with black paint. Make black-and-white photocopies of clip art or photographs, reducing them to fit within the frames. Glue the artwork into the frames. Slide narrow black ribbons through the frame hooks or hangers, and tie them around rolled napkins. **NOTE:** If the frame does not have a hanger on the back, make one by gluing a loop of narrow ribbon to the back of the frame.

bonjour!

❧ Chalkboards often display the daily special at a bistro. Here they serve as an anchor for each table's centerpiece. Paint wooden plaques with blackboard paint, write a French phrase on each, then place Parisian souvenirs on the chalkboard. Add a handcrafted lavender topiary as a final salute to France.

chair frames

❧ Sand unfinished 4×6-inch wooden frames (available at crafts or discount stores). Paint all sides with two or more coats of black paint. Cut decorative papers, photocopies of photographs, or clip art to float within the frame or gather scrapbooking or souvenir trinkets to dangle in the frames. If the papers are thin, glue them to cardstock or hang tags. Attach the center items to the frames with ribbon. Glue a ribbon loop to the upper corners of each frame. Hang the frames from an S hook on the chair back covers. See the photograph *above* for details on hanging the frames.

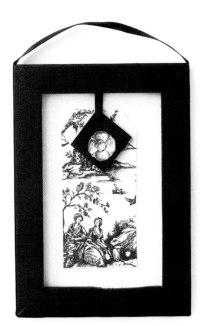

chalkboard centerpiece

1 Sand and prime purchased wooden plaques. Rub the primed surface with a brown paper bag so the surface is completely smooth. Paint the boards with two or more coats of blackboard paint following the paint manufacturer's instructions and sanding between coats.

2 Using chalk or a chalk pencil, write a simple French phrase across each board. See below for suggestions or check bilingual dictionaries or online translation guides. Place French souvenirs and a lavender topiary on each board.

108

TRANSLATIONS:
Happy New Year
Nouvelle Année Heureuse

•

good friends
bon amis

•

celebrate
célébrez

•

love
amour

•

wealth
richesse

•

happiness
bonheur

•

health
santé

•

lavender topiary

1. Brush a small green plastic foam ball with tacky white crafts glue.
NOTE: If a green ball is not available, spray paint the ball with green paint appropriate for plastic foam. Roll the ball in lavender buds until it is completely coated. Set the ball aside.

2. Paint a terra-cotta flowerpot black and a dowel green. (The sizes of the pot and dowel depend on the size of the ball and the overall topiary.) When all the components are dry, wedge florist's foam into the pot. Push one end of the dowel into the ball and the other into the pot. Cover the florist's foam with moss. If desired, glue a band of ribbon to the rim of the pot.

Cashew-Caramel
Meringues

Cashew-Caramel Meringues

❋

The contrasting duo of rich, luscious ice cream against crisp, airy meringues shows up often in French desserts— to sublime effects.

 2 egg whites
 ⅛ teaspoon cream of tartar
 ½ cup sugar
 ½ cup chopped cashews or
     mixed nuts
 1 to 2 tablespoons chopped
     cashews or mixed
     nuts (optional)
 1 pint premium chocolate, coffee,
     or vanilla ice cream
 1 recipe Homemade
     Caramel Sauce
     Sweetened whipped
     cream (optional)

Place egg whites in a large mixing bowl and let stand at room temperature for 30 minutes.

Preheat oven to 300°F. Line baking sheets with clean plain brown paper or parchment paper. Draw eight 3-inch circles on the paper; set aside.

Add cream of tartar to egg whites; beat with an electric mixer on medium speed until soft peaks form (tips curl). Add sugar, 1 tablespoon at a time, beating on high speed for 4 to 5 minutes until stiff peaks form (tips stand straight) and sugar is almost dissolved. Stir in the ½ cup cashews.

Using the back of a spoon, spread the egg white mixture over the circles, slightly building up the sides. If desired, sprinkle with the 1 to 2 tablespoons chopped nuts.

Bake for 35 minutes. Turn off oven. Let meringues dry in oven, with door closed, for 1 hour. Carefully remove from paper. Cool completely on wire rack.

To serve, place a scoop of ice cream in each meringue. Drizzle with Homemade Caramel Sauce. If desired, dollop with whipped cream. Makes 8 servings.

TO MAKE AHEAD: Prepare and bake meringues as directed. Place completely cooled meringues in a covered container; store at room temperature for up to 3 days. Serve as directed above.

HOMEMADE CARAMEL SAUCE: In a heavy medium saucepan stir together ¾ cup packed brown sugar; ½ cup whipping cream; ½ cup butter, softened; and 2 tablespoons light-colored corn syrup. Bring to boiling over medium-high heat, whisking occasionally; reduce heat to medium. Boil gently for 3 minutes. Stir in ½ teaspoon vanilla. Let cool for 15 to 30 minutes before using. Makes 1½ cups sauce.

wines for your bistro table

Because the French often label their wines by region rather than grape, choosing a wine you like can be hard. Rather than thinking of Chardonnay, Merlot, or Shiraz, think in terms of regions, such as Burgundy or the Loire Valley. Here's what to consider.

■ Alsace: Riesling reigns here. Ask your wine merchant to steer you toward drier versions of Riesling from Alsace. If you love a little spice and a hint of sweetness, try a Gewürztraminer. To kick off this New Year's Eve menu, offer your guests an aperitif of either a dry Riesling or a sweeter Gewürztraminer.

■ Bordeaux: The famous dry reds here blend Cabernet Sauvignon, Merlot, Cabernet Franc, Malbec, and Petit Verdot. A wine merchant can guide you to those that are more Merlot-based or Cabernet-based if you wish. Bordeaux whites aren't as well-known as the reds, but well worth trying.

■ Burgundy (Bourgogne): Pinot Noir is Burgundy's famous red grape. Expect

French versions to be less fruity than their American counterparts. White wines from Burgundy are almost always made from Chardonnay and are generally more fruity. Many people feel they don't measure up well to the California Chardonnays. If you like fruity reds, try Beaujolais made from the Gamay grape. Beaujolais is also a good introduction to red wine. Either a Pinot Noir-based Burgundy or a Beaujolais would go well with the turkey entrée featured in this menu.

■ Champagne: Champagne—from the Champagne region of France—can be made from Chardonnay, Pinot Noir, or Pinot Meunière grapes and often can be a bit pricey. For a more affordable choice, toast in the New Year with the sparkling wines from the Loire Valley. Though they're usually less expensive than traditional champagnes, most are made in the same method as the so still provide an elegant sip.

■ Languedoc-Roussillon: To serve a crowd on a budget, seek out affordable wines labeled Vin de Pays d'Oc. These wines often are labeled by grape—find Cabernet Sauvignon, Merlot, Syrah, and Chardonnay from this region.

Loire: If you like dry, elegant Sauvignon Blancs, reach for Sancerre and Pouilly-Fumé. A sweeter style of Vouvray is made from Chenin Blanc. Also try sparkling wines from the Loire Valley.

■ Rhône: The Syrah grape stars in the powerful red wines from the northern Rhône; look for Côte Rôtie, Hermitage, and Crozes-Hermitage. In the southern Rhône, you'll find food-friendly blends. For a splurge, reach for a Châteauneuf-du-Pape. A Syrah-based wine from the northern Rhône would pair nicely with the lamb entrée.

glass slipper

 A slide-on cover, often called a "slipper," serves as an on-the-go coaster.

■ Trace the foot of the stemware onto paper; add ½ inch all around and cut out the pattern. Using plain or decorative-edge scissors, cut out a felt circle for each glass. Cut a second circle from patterned oilcloth, making it ¼ inch smaller all around than the first circle. If oilcloth is not available, fuse lightweight interfacing to the back of

cotton fabric to prevent the edges from fraying. On each patterned circle, cut a line from the outer edge to the center.

■ Turn the wine glass upside down and measure the diameter of the stem where it joins the base. Cut a circle this size in the center of each of the patterned circles.

■ Center a patterned circle over a felt circle. Join the two halfway around the outer edges with stitching or fabric glue. Leave the edge with the slit open. See the

photograph *right* for details. Repeat for each set of circles. To use the slipper, slide the foot of the stemware between the layers of fabric so it fits snugly around the foot of the glass. See the photograph *above* for details.

give than receive. Create quick and simple custom-designed gifts for everyone on your list. Add beads to purchased items, embellish treasures found at the discount store, or make something special for the guys in your life. It's easy to make something for everyone.

GIVING
from the HEART

girlfriends cookie

& gift exchange

You've shared laughs and tears, good times and maybe a few bad ones with your girlfriends. Now it's time to share cookies and gifts—and another good time.

Gingered Cranberry-Orange Balls

girlfriend take-and-bake day

Celebrate your friendships with a cookie and gift exchange that transforms two dozen of one kind of cookie into two dozen cookies of all kinds. It's not magic; it's math. Have every guest bring two and a half dozen cookies and a take-home container. As each friend arrives, put out six of her cookies to snack on and set the other two dozen aside (except for the Roly-Poly Snowfolk). As gifts and laughs are exchanged, the cookies become the party treats alongside coffee, tea, cocoa, or your favorite beverage. At the end of the party, everyone fills her container with two dozen cookies from the overall mix.

To make both the baking and crafting easier, look to the following pages for recipes and craft projects that can be made in multiples. Using a single dough, you can make three different cookies. Employ one crafting technique, alter each gift a bit, and you've made personalized gifts assembly-line style. Both the recipes and crafts are so simple, you'll want to make them for more than just your girlfriends.

Gingered Cranberry-Orange Balls

Fruit and nuts, imbued with a snappy ginger flavor and glazed in a white coating, will make these no-bake balls a standout at your cookie exchange.

    1 6-ounce package dried
          cranberries
    1 16-ounce box gingersnaps,
          finely crushed
 1¾ cups ground toasted pecans
          or walnuts
    ⅓ cup powdered sugar
    1 tablespoon finely shredded
          orange peel
    ½ cup orange juice
    ⅓ cup butter, melted
    2 tablespoons very finely chopped
          crystallized ginger
 2½ cups white baking pieces
    1 tablespoon shortening

Line two large cookie sheets with waxed paper; set aside. Finely snip ⅓ cup of the dried cranberries; set aside. Coarsely snip the remaining cranberries.

In a large bowl combine the coarsely snipped cranberries, crushed gingersnaps, ground pecans, powdered sugar, and orange peel. Add orange juice and melted butter; stir until well mixed. Shape mixture into 1-inch balls. Place balls onto the prepared cookie sheets; let stand about 1 hour or until dry. In a small bowl combine the finely snipped cranberries and crystallized ginger; set aside.

For coating, in a small heavy saucepan combine baking pieces and shortening. Cook and stir over medium-low heat until melted. Remove from heat. Dip balls in the melted mixture, turning each ball to coat completely. Return coated balls to cookie sheets. Sprinkle with cranberry-ginger mixture. Let stand for 15 to 30 minutes or until coating is set. Makes about 60 balls.

Coffee-and-Cream Sandwich Cookies

Basic Dough

One dough—three cookies: That's the concept of this multipurpose recipe, which you can morph into Coffee-and-Cream Sandwich Cookies, Fruity Almond Thumbprints, or Roly-Poly Snowfolk.

½ cup butter, softened
½ cup shortening
1 cup sugar
1 teaspoon baking powder
¼ teaspoon salt
1 egg
1 teaspoon vanilla
2¼ cups all-purpose flour

In a large mixing bowl beat butter and shortening with an electric mixer on medium to high speed for 30 seconds. Add sugar, baking powder, and salt. Beat until combined, scraping sides of bowl occasionally. Beat in egg and vanilla until combined. Beat in as much of the flour as you can with the mixer. Using a wooden spoon, stir in any remaining flour.

Use dough as directed in individual recipes at *right* and on *page 118*.

TO STORE: Prepare dough as directed. Pack dough into an airtight freezer container. Seal, label, and freeze for up to 1 month. Thaw in the refrigerator overnight before using.

Coffee-and-Cream Sandwich Cookies

Choose this recipe if you want to transform the basic dough into a sophisticated, coffeehouse-worthy cookie.

1 recipe Basic Dough (*left*)
2 cups powdered sugar
2 tablespoons butter, softened
2 teaspoons instant espresso powder or instant coffee crystals
1 teaspoon vanilla
  Half-and-half, light cream, or milk
1 tablespoon unsweetened cocoa powder or 1 ounce semisweet or bittersweet chocolate, melted

Prepare Basic Dough; divide dough in half. Cover and chill for 2 to 3 hours or until dough is easy to handle.

Preheat oven to 375°F. On a lightly floured surface, roll dough to ⅛-inch thickness. Using desired 1½-inch cookie cutter, cut out dough, dipping cutter into flour between cuts. Place cutouts 2 inches apart onto an ungreased cookie sheet. Bake for 8 to 10 minutes or until edges are lightly browned. Transfer cookies to a wire rack and let cool.

For filling, in a small bowl stir together powdered sugar, butter, espresso powder, and vanilla; stir in enough half-and-half to make a spreadable filling. Spread 1 teaspoon of the filling onto the bottoms of half of the cookies. Top each spread cookie with a remaining cookie, bottom side down. Place cocoa powder in a small sieve and sift over filled cookies or drizzle melted chocolate over cookies. Makes about 40 sandwich cookies.

TO STORE: Place filled cookies in layers separated by waxed paper in an airtight container; cover. Store at room temperature for up to 3 days. (Or freeze unfilled cookies in freezer container for up to 3 months. Thaw cookies; fill and assemble as directed.)

117

Fruity Almond Thumbprints

Roly-Poly Snowfolk

Fruity Almond Thumbprints

Thumbprint cookies are a Christmastime classic. This one uses fruit curd or pie filling for luscious sweet-tart centers.

1 recipe Basic Dough
  (recipe, *page 117*)
1 slightly beaten egg white
1 cup finely chopped almonds
  Purchased lemon curd or cherry
  pie filling

Preheat oven to 375°F. Lightly grease a cookie sheet; set aside. Prepare Basic Dough. Shape dough into 1-inch balls. Roll balls in egg white, then in almonds. Place balls 2 inches apart onto prepared cookie sheet. Press your thumb into the center of each ball.

Bake for 8 to 10 minutes or until edges are lightly browned. Press puffed centers down using the rounded side of a measuring tablespoon. Transfer cookies to a wire rack and let cool.

Just before serving, fill center of each cookie with about 1½ teaspoons lemon curd or pie filling. Makes about 42.

TO STORE: Place cookies in layers separated by waxed paper in an airtight container; cover. Store in the refrigerator for up to 3 days. (Or freeze unfilled cookies in freezer container for up to 3 months. Thaw cookies; fill as directed.)

Roly-Poly Snowfolk

Your friends who have children will enjoy taking these playful characters home to their kids.

1 recipe Basic Dough
  (recipe, *page 117*)
  Miniature candy-coated milk
    chocolate pieces or other
    small candies
  Miniature semisweet
    chocolate pieces
  Crafts sticks (optional)
1 recipe Gumdrop Hats
1 recipe Gumdrop Scarves
  Canned vanilla frosting

Preheat oven to 350°F. Prepare Basic Dough. Shape dough into ten 1½-inch balls, ten 1-inch balls, and ten ¾-inch balls (30 balls total).

For each snowfolk, arrange a 1½-inch ball, a 1-inch ball, and a ¾-inch ball about ½ inch apart on an ungreased cookie sheet. Slightly flatten the 1½-inch ball. Press miniature candy-coated pieces or other candies into the 1½-inch ball and the 1-inch ball for buttons; press miniature semisweet pieces into the ¾-inch balls for eyes. If desired, insert a crafts stick into each 1½-inch ball. Build snowfolk 2 inches apart on cookie sheet.

Bake for 12 to 15 minutes or until edges are lightly browned. Let stand for 2 minutes on the cookie sheet. Carefully transfer snowfolk to a wire rack and let cool. (Do not pick up by sticks, if using, until cookies are completely cool.) Attach Gumdrop Hats and Gumdrop Scarves to snowfolk with canned frosting. Makes 10 snowfolk.

GUMDROP HATS: Sprinkle a cutting board with granulated sugar. Place one large gumdrop onto board and sprinkle with more sugar. With a rolling pin, roll gumdrop into an oval about ¼ inch thick. Curve to form a hat and press edges together to seal. If desired, bend up gumdrop edge for brim. Repeat to make 10 hats.

GUMDROP SCARVES: Sprinkle a cutting board with granulated sugar. Place one large gumdrop onto board and sprinkle with more sugar. With a rolling pin, roll gumdrop into an oval about ¼ inch thick. Cut oval into strips with a knife or scissors. Snip slits in one end of each strip for fringe. Repeat to make a total of 20 strips. For each scarf, crisscross two strips, fringe ends down.

TO STORE: Place cookies in layers separated by waxed paper in an airtight container; cover. Store at room temperature for up to 3 days. (Or freeze in freezer container for up to 3 months.)

Chocolate-
Coconut Bars

Peppermint Stars

Chocolate-Coconut Bars

1 4-ounce package sweet
   baking chocolate
⅔ cup butter or margarine
¾ cup granulated sugar
½ cup packed brown sugar
2 eggs
½ teaspoon vanilla
1 cup all-purpose flour
1 cup chopped almonds, toasted
1 recipe Coconut Topping

Preheat oven to 325°F. Line a
13×9×2-inch baking pan with foil; extend
foil over edges of pan. Grease foil.

In a large microwave-safe bowl
combine chocolate and butter. Cover bowl
with plastic wrap, turning back one section
to vent. Microwave on 100 percent power
(high) about 1½ minutes or until almost
melted; stir until smooth. Using a wooden
spoon, stir in granulated sugar, brown sugar,
eggs, and vanilla until smooth. Stir in flour
and ¼ teaspoon *salt.* Spread evenly into
prepared pan. Sprinkle with almonds.

Spread Coconut Topping evenly over
chocolate layer. Bake for 45 to
50 minutes or until golden brown and
just set in the middle. If necessary to
prevent overbrowning, cover with foil
for the last 10 minutes of baking. Cool
completely in pan on a wire rack.

To cut, lift bars out of pan with foil. Peel
off foil and cut into bars. Makes 42 bars.
COCONUT TOPPING: In a bowl
whisk together ½ cup granulated sugar,
1 egg, 1 tablespoon all-purpose flour,
½ teaspoon baking powder, and ½
teaspoon vanilla. Stir in one 7-ounce bag
shredded coconut.

TO STORE: Prepare and bake as
directed. Cover and freeze for up to 1
week. Thaw at room temperature.

Peppermint Stars

½ cup butter, softened
1 cup sugar
1 teaspoon baking powder
¼ teaspoon baking soda
¼ teaspoon salt
½ cup dairy sour cream
1 egg
½ teaspoon peppermint extract
2½ cups all-purpose flour
1 recipe Peppermint Icing
1 drop red food coloring
   Finely crushed peppermint
   candy canes

Preheat oven to 375°F. In a large
mixing bowl beat butter with an electric
mixer on medium to high speed for
30 seconds. Add sugar, baking powder,
baking soda, and salt. Beat until combined,
scraping sides of bowl occasionally. Beat in
sour cream, egg, and peppermint extract
until combined. Beat in as much of the
flour as you can with the mixer. Using a
wooden spoon, stir in any remaining flour.

Divide dough in half. Cover and chill
dough for 1 to 2 hours or until easy to handle.

On a well-floured surface, roll out
dough, half at a time, to ¼-inch thickness.
Using a 2½- to 3-inch star-shape cookie
cutter, cut out dough, dipping cutter into
flour between cuts. Place cutouts 1 inch
apart onto ungreased cookie sheets.

Bake for 6 to 7 minutes or until edges
are firm and bottoms are lightly browned.
Transfer to a wire rack and let cool.

Transfer half of the Peppermint Icing
to another bowl. Stir the red food coloring
into one portion of the icing, making it
pink. Drizzle cookies with pink and white
icings, and sprinkle with finely crushed
candy canes. Let stand until icing is set.
Makes about 42 cookies.

PEPPERMINT ICING: In a medium
bowl stir together 2 cups powdered sugar,
2 tablespoons milk, and ¼ teaspoon
peppermint extract. Stir in enough
additional milk, 1 teaspoon at a time, to
make a drizzling consistency.

TO STORE: Place undrizzled cookies
in layers separated by waxed paper in an
airtight container; cover. Store at room
temperature for up to 3 days. (Or freeze
in freezer container for up to 3 months.
Thaw cookies.) Drizzle with icing and
sprinkle with candy canes as directed.

119

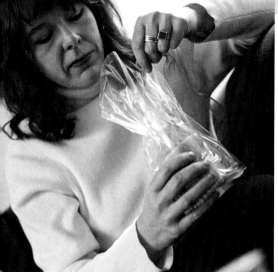

girlfriends gift exchange

COOL IT

Keep beverages cool in definite "girly" style. Cover plain foam drink holders with fabric, then add beads, ribbons, and other glam trims. For more ideas, see *page 154*.

1 Cut the fabric 1 inch wider than the height of the holder and 1 inch longer than the circumference. Press under ½ inch on both long edges and ½ inch on one short edge. If necessary, glue the hems in place.

2 *Squeeze glue* over the outside of the holder, then spread it smooth with the brush. Wrap the fabric around the holder, smoothing and pressing it into place and keeping the edges aligned. Glue the hemmed short edge over the starting point so all the edges are finished.

3 *Glue layers of trims* to the top and bottom edges, turning raw edges under.

MAKE THEIR MARK

Three simple items—ribbons, eyelets, and beads—form easy but elegant bookmarks. Make each bookmark unique by layering together different colors and patterns of ribbons and selecting a variety of beads. For more ideas, see *page 156*.

1 Cut the ribbons to the desired length. To seal the edges and prevent fraying, use a woodburning tool to "cut" the ribbon or apply fray-checking liquid to cut edges.

2 Glue the ribbons one atop the other to create the desired pattern. Ribbons can be centered or offset.

3 After the glue dries, insert one or more eyelets in each end of the bookmark. NOTE: You may have to cut through the layers of ribbon first in order to insert the eyelet.

4 Thread the beads onto the head pins. Make a loop at the end. Use a jump ring to attach the bead strand to the eyelet.

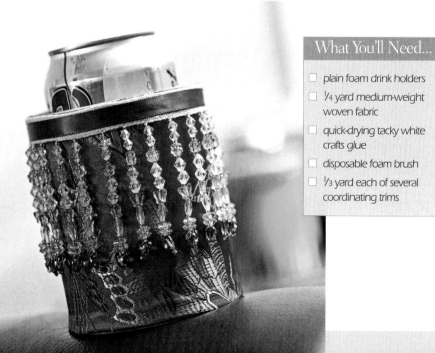

What You'll Need...

- [ ] pillar candle
- [ ] large rubber bands
- [ ] sequin pins
- [ ] flat, faceted, or shaped sequins in various sizes
- [ ] various beads
- [ ] candle plate or glass coaster
- [ ] ribbon
- [ ] additional matching beads for wrapping
- [ ] matches (optional)

BEADS OF LIGHT

Make an inexpensive pillar candle sparkle like a bejeweled masterpiece by using sequin pins to add beads and sequins. Color is the key to personalizing each candle.

1 To mark straight lines for the beaded decorations, place rubber bands around the candle. Measure from the bottom or top to make sure the rubber bands run parallel and evenly around the candle.

2 Slide a bead and sequin onto a sequin pin, then push the pin into the candle. Continue around the candle creating an even design. NOTE: If a pin has to be repositioned, fill the hole by quickly passing a lit match over it until the surrounding wax fills the hole.

3 Place the finished candle on a glass candle plate or coaster. Wrap ribbon around the candle. Add additional beads to the ribbon.

What You'll Need...

FOR APPROXIMATELY TEN
8-OUNCE GIFTS:

☐ 10 cups sea salt

☐ 2 cups baking soda

☐ essential oils such as rose, lavender, peppermint, or other desired scents

FOR THE DECANTERS:

☐ clear glass bottles with corks or stoppers

☐ thin wire

☐ various beads

☐ ribbon scrap

☐ button

☐ decorative paper scraps

BATHING BEAUTY
SCENTED BATH SALTS

～ Let your friends soak up a pretty scent with handmade bath salts. Essential oil makes it possible to vary the fragrance of the basic potion. A decorated decanter makes the gift even more special.

FOR THE BATH SALTS

1 Mix the dry salt and soda in a large container. Add approximately 20 drops of the desired essential oil one drop at a time. Adjust the amount as needed. For lavender rose, use 10 drops of lavender oil and 10 drops of rose oil. Mix the oil in with your fingers.

2 To use the salts, add approximately ½ cup to drawn bath water.

FOR THE DECANTER

1 Tightly wrap wire around the neck of the bottle, leaving a tail at each end. Tie the ends in a square knot at the center front of the wrapping. Curl the ends around a pencil or dowel. Cut two additional lengths of wire. Make a small loop at one end of each wire, then string beads onto the wires. Fasten the wires to the knot.

2 Loop ribbon around the bottles. See the photograph *above* for details. Sew a button to the ribbons where they overlap.

3 Cut a small piece of plain paper for the label and write the name of the salt on it. Cut a slightly larger piece of decorative paper and glue the label to this backing paper. Cut a third piece of paper slightly smaller than the decorative paper. Layer the tag, ribbon, and final paper together and glue them in place so the ribbon is sandwiched between the papers.

NAP OF LUXURY

〜 Handpainted linens cost a bundle at boutiques. Make your own for a fraction of the cost using rubber fabric stamps or precut stencils. Vary the colors and designs to match your friends' decor.

1 *Wash and dry the napkins.* Do not use fabric softener or detergent with additives. Iron smooth.

2 *Mix the paints with textile medium* according to the manufacturer's directions.

For stenciled napkins: Position the stencil over the napkin. Dip the tip of the stencil brush into the desired paint. Tap the brush onto the plate to remove most of the paint. Stencil the desired areas using a scrubbing motion. Repeat for the other colors, using a new brush for each color.
For painted borders: Using a foam brush, paint the hem using the stitching line as a guide. Because of the handpainted nature, the strokes may be uneven.
For stamped napkins: Using the foam brush, lightly paint each section of the stamp with the appropriate color paint. Carefully press the stamp onto the napkin. Repeat as necessary to cover either one corner or the entire napkin.

TEA TIME

〜 Personalize a plain glass mug with an etched initial. Glass etching cream and purchased letters from the scrapbooking aisle make it easy to form the design. Add a few tea bags and some ribbon for a pretty presentation.

1 *Thoroughly wash and dry the mug,* then wipe the outside surface with vinegar to remove any residue.

2 *Press a self-adhesive letter* to the outside of the mug at the desired height. To create the frosted window, tape off a square or rectangle around the letter. Burnish down the edges of the tape and letter with the handle of the paintbrush.

3 *Wearing gloves* and using a foam brush, apply etching cream inside the taped window and over the letter following the manufacturer's directions. Let the etching cream work, then wash it off. Remove the tape and letter.

4 *To make the tag,* cut a smaller tag from plain card stock and a slightly larger tag from decorative paper. See the photograph *above* for details. Glue the papers together. Punch a hole at center top and center bottom.

5 *Tie the ribbon* around the tea bags and knot it at the center in an overhand knot. Slide the ribbon ends through the holes in the tags and knot the ends. See the photograph *above* for details.

123

the bead goes on

Boxes, bags, clothing, and lamps—everything is better when beads are added.

What You'll Need...

- ☐ wicker storage baskets
- ☐ acrylic paint and bristle-style paintbrush (optional)
- ☐ coordinating fringes, ribbons, and beaded trims
- ☐ hot-glue gun and glue sticks

on the fringe

Band storage baskets with beaded fringe and they go from functional to fantastic. These boxes are open but their lidded counterparts work just as well with the trims applied to the lip of the lid.

1 If desired, paint the inside and outside of the baskets with one or two coats.

2 Select two or more trims to layer onto each basket. Starting with the trim that will be in the background, glue the trim to the basket edge. Turn under the raw edge, where the beginning and ending overlap. Add the remaining rows of trim in the same manner.

basket case

Whether it holds silk flowers, winter's greens, correspondence, or even work files, a simple wall basket takes on a look of importance when trimmed with ribbon and beads.

1 Starting and ending at the back, glue the beaded trim around the basket. Allow space above the trim for the ribbon plus about 1 inch of wicker.

2 Glue the ribbon over the flange edge of the bead trim, turning under the raw edge at the back.

What You'll Need...

- ☐ wicker wall basket
- ☐ beaded dingleberry trim with a flange edge
- ☐ ribbon
- ☐ hot-glue gun and glue sticks

What You'll Need...

- [ ] plain purchased shade
- [ ] ruler or tape measure
- [ ] wide (approximately ⅝ inches wide) and narrow (approximately ⅜ inches wide) coordinating ribbons
- [ ] clear fast-drying fabric glue
- [ ] clip-style clothespins
- [ ] awl and hammer
- [ ] scrapbooking brads
- [ ] medium-weight (approximately 14-gauge) silver wire
- [ ] wire cutters
- [ ] acrylic prisms (see *page 128* for sources)
- [ ] needle-nose pliers

catch the light

 A shade embellished with ribbon trim and large dangling prisms turns a bargain-basement lamp into a boutique-quality accent.

1 Mark equidistant points along the top and bottom edges of the lampshade. Connect the points with a light pencil line, forming an X pattern around the shade.

2 Working in one direction at a time, glue the wide ribbon over the lines. Trim the ends and glue them to the inside of the shade. Hold the ribbon in place with clothespins until the glue dries. Center the narrow ribbon over the wide ribbon and glue it in place. After the glue dries, repeat the process in the other direction to complete the X patterns. See the photograph *opposite* for details.

3 Using an awl, make a small hole in the center of each ribbon X. Insert a small brad into each hole.

4 Using the awl, make evenly spaced holes for the prisms along the lower edge of the lampshade. Cut the wire to 4-inch lengths. Insert the wire through the prism and make a loop to hold it in place. Curve the wire into an S shape and insert the remaining end through the hole in the shade. Trim the wire to the desired length, depending on the size of your prism. See the photograph *right* for details. Loop the end back on itself to secure it.

What You'll Need...

- [ ] small plain shoulder bag
- [ ] beaded rope (available at fabric stores; it may have a flange edge that can be cut away)
- [ ] scrapbooking ribbon labels with loop ends for ribbon
- [ ] ribbon to fit the scrapbooking trims
- [ ] clear-drying permanent flexible fabric glue
- [ ] beaded fringe with a flange edge

bedazzling bag

 Ribbons, scrapbooking trims, and beaded rope and fringe turn a plain shoulder bag into one worthy of an evening on the town.

1 Remove the original purse shoulder strap and replace it with the beaded rope.

2 Glue a row of ribbon and one ribbon label to the top edge of the purse, turning the raw edges of the ribbon under. Repeat for a second row of ribbon and another ribbon label.

3 Glue a row of beaded fringe below the ribbon rows. Cover the flange on the fringe with a third row of ribbon and a final ribbon label.

dashing danglers

〜 Perk up a plain poncho with large colorful prisms. Look for colored prisms in with holiday trims, package wrappings, and lighting accessories at gift, crafts, and decorating stores.

1 Attach each prism to a jump or split ring. Jump rings are easier to use but split rings are more secure.

2 Sew the rings to the poncho, spacing the prisms evenly. To avoid damaging the prisms, hand-wash the poncho.

easy elegance

∿ Bead shops and departments abound, making it possible to match a necklace to any outfit. Start with our basic directions for making a two-strand necklace, then alter them to fit the beads that catch your eye.

1 Determine the desired length of both strands. Knot the end of the beading thread. Place the ball hook over the knot. Using the flat-nosed pliers, pinch it in one direction. Turn it 90 degrees and pinch again. This will encase the knot in a crimped square.

2 Slide the beads onto the beading thread in the desired order. For interest, alter the sizes and colors of the beads by dividing them into sections. See the photograph *right* for ideas on arranging the beads.

3 When you reach the center, add the pendant. To create the pendant, place a small bead, the pendant bead, and another small bead on the head pin. If necessary, cut the excess length from the head pin. Using the round-nose pliers, make a loop for hanging just above the top bead. String the pendant onto the necklace.

129

4 String the remaining beads onto the thread so they are symmetrical with the first side. Knot the thread at the end and cover the knot with a ball hook.

5 Create the second smaller strand in the same manner, but place a different-color or larger bead in the center of the strand in place of a pendant.

6 Lay out the necklace. On one end join the two hook ends of the ball rings to a jump ring, folding the hooks over the jump ring. Repeat for the other end. Attach the rings to the loops of the toggle clasp. See the photograph *right* for details.

making cents

Discount and dollar stores hold untold treasures-in-the-making.

With a little imagination, the simplest of objects can be transformed into spectacular gifts. Check the basic materials found for a dollar or less, then see how they were transformed with basic crafting techniques and materials. Use these ideas as inspiration for thrifty gifts of your own.

painted dinnerware

Transform clear glass dinnerware into works of art by painting it with simple designs. Stickers and stick-on letters provide a guide for the pattern.

FOR EACH PLATE, BOWL, OR WINE GLASS

NOTE: All the painting is done on the wrong side of the bowl and plate. For the stemware, paint on the right side but keep all paint from the upper 1 inch of the rim.

1 Wash the glass in warm soapy water, rinse with vinegar, and dry thoroughly. This will remove any residue. Take care when handling the glassware so fingerprints and other residue do not keep the paint from adhering.

2 Place the letters on the right side of the plate or bowl, spelling out the desired phrases. Place the sticker on the right side.

3 Turn the plate or bowl over and using a paint pen, trace the letters and the outline of the heart. Let the paint dry and trace over it again or touch it up with a brush if needed. Let dry completely. Remove the letters and stickers.

4 On the wrong side, paint over the outlined sections, covering the letters and filling in the heart shape.

5 Make brushstrokes that radiate out from the center of the bowl, the remaining sections of the plate rim, or up the bowl and along the foot of the stemware. Add dots using the handle end of the paintbrush. Let dry.

6 Fill in the remaining sections with the desired paint colors. Let dry completely.

7 Following the paint manufacturer's instructions, seal the paint, cure it, or bake it to make it permanent. (Different brands of paint have different curing processes. Follow the directions exactly.)

What You'll Need...

- [ ] clear glass plates, bowls, and stemware
- [ ] vinegar
- [ ] self-adhesive letters and heart-shape stickers
- [ ] paint pens for glass
- [ ] glass paint in the desired colors and glass paint sealer (if recommended by the paint manufacturer)
- [ ] flat and round paintbrushes

What You'll Need...

FOR ALL PROJECTS:

☐ plain lampshade

☐ hot-glue gun and glue sticks

FOR THE RIBBON SHADE:

☐ sheer green ribbon, about 1 inch wide

☐ sheer orange ribbon, about 3 inches wide

☐ shank-style buttons

☐ needle-nose pliers

☐ ½-inch-wide ribbon to match the shade

FOR THE DECOUPAGE PRINT AND BUTTON SHADE:

☐ decoupage paper and decorative papers

☐ decorative-edge scissors

☐ decoupage medium

☐ disposable foam brush

☐ buttons

FOR THE FLOWER SHADE:

☐ embroidered flower patches

☐ artist's acrylic paint and flat paintbrush

☐ bangle-style ribbon fringe

looking for shade

🌊 Give personality to a plain paper or fabric lampshade with simple embellishments you can find at crafts and fabrics stores.

FOR THE RIBBON SHADE

1 Divide the top and bottom edges of the shade into even intervals. Cut the narrow sheer ribbon 1 inch longer than the height of the shade. Hot-glue the narrow ribbon to the shade at every marking so it runs in vertical lines. Place the glue at the top and bottom edges only, turning those edges to the inside. Trim away the excess ribbon.

2 Cut the wide sheer ribbon 2 inches longer than the height of the shade, cutting twice as many wide strips as there are narrow strips.

3 Place 2 wide strips together. Using the pliers and taking care not to damage the ribbon, draw the ribbon through the button shank and slide the button to the middle of the ribbons. Repeat for each set of ribbons. Fan out the ribbons to form a wide strip and glue the upper and lower edges to the top and bottom of the shade on the inside. See the photograph *top left* for details. Trim away the excess ribbon.

4 Glue the matching ribbon to the inside of the shade to cover the raw edges of the sheer ribbons.

FOR THE DECOUPAGE PRINT SHADE

1 Cut out the desired designs from the decoupage paper. Cut decorative papers to layer under the decoupage papers and for a band around the lower edge.

2 Brush decoupage medium to the back side of the papers and use it as glue

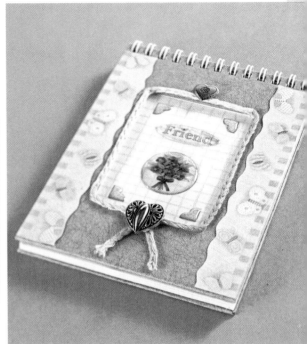

to hold the papers to the shade. Layer the papers as desired, gluing each layer separately. Paint the shade with three or more coats of decoupage medium.

3️⃣ Glue buttons to the shade.

FOR THE FLOWER SHADE

1️⃣ Glue the flowers to the shade, scattering them randomly but evenly.

2️⃣ Paint small rectangles along the top and bottom edges of the shade.

3️⃣ Glue bangle fringe to the inside of the shade so the ribbon does not show but the bangles hang freely.

something noteworthy

🌀 Turn a plain little notebook into a personalized journal by adding papers, buttons, and trims.

1️⃣ If the notebook has a window, remove the window piece. Cut decorative paper to fit the notebook front. Using paper glue, glue it to the inside so the decorative side shows through the window. If the notebook does not have a window, cut a piece of paper to fit over the center of the notebook and glue it in place. Decorate the center section with stickers or other scrapbooking trims.

2️⃣ Cut bands of paper to fit the outer edges of the notebook and glue them in place as borders for the notebook.

3️⃣ Using tacky glue, add buttons, ribbons, and other trims as desired.

What You'll Need...

- ☐ notebook with or without a window
- ☐ various decorative papers
- ☐ decorative-edge scissors
- ☐ paper glue and tacky glue
- ☐ stickers, buttons, yarn, and scrapbooking trims as desired

133

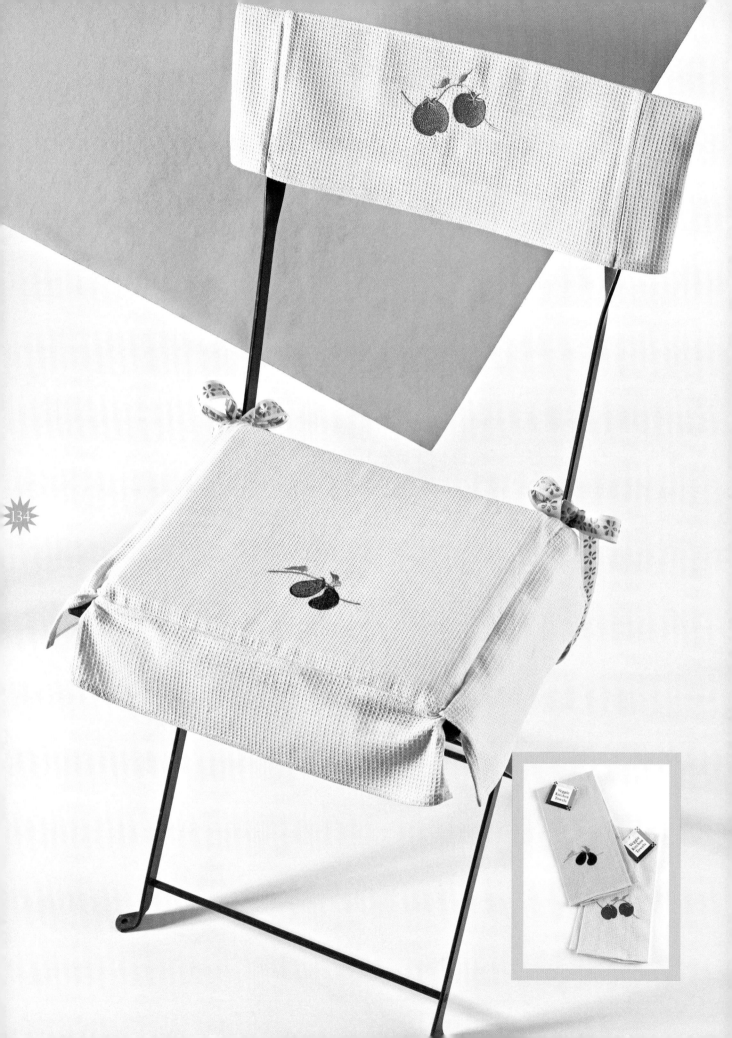

What You'll Need...

- ☐ large paper for patterns
- ☐ 2 kitchen towels large enough to cover the chair seat and back
- ☐ 1-inch-deep upholstery foam to fit the chair seat
- ☐ ribbon for ties

give it the slip

❧ Perk up plain folding chairs with slipcovers made from embroidered waffle-weave towels. Look for heavy towels with a single bold motif.

NOTE: Always make the most of both the towel design and the hemmed edges. When cutting out the pieces, position your pattern so it first falls where the design looks best and then, if possible, where there is a prehemmed edge. If there is not a prehemmed edge, add ½ inch to that side and narrowly hem the fabric before sewing it to the remaining pieces.

1 Trace the seat dimensions and back dimensions onto paper for the patterns. For the seat, add 1 inch to each side and cut out the pattern. Cut a seat front and a seat back from one towel.

2 For the chair skirt, cut 4½-inch-wide pieces to fit the front and each side using a different-color towel. With right sides facing, sew the skirt pieces to the front and sides of the chair seat piece using ½-inch seam allowances.

3 Fold the skirt pieces toward the center of the seat piece, keeping them free from the stitching lines. Place the seat back over the seat front, right sides facing and the skirt pieces encased. Sew around all the edges, leaving the back open. Clip the corners and trim the seam allowances.

4 Turn the seat cover to the right side. Insert the foam and slip-stitch the opening closed. Tack ribbon ties to the back corners.

5 For the back slipcover, cut 2 inches off each short end of the pattern. Discard one short pattern piece. Add ½ inch to one long side and both short sides of the big piece; add ½ inch to both long sides and one short side of the small pattern piece.

6 Fold the remaining towel fabric in half, right sides facing. Cut the big piece from the seat's skirt material, placing one long edge on the fold. Cut two short pieces from the seat's main fabric, placing one short edge along the folded edge.

7 Sew the long edge of a short piece to one short edge of the big piece. Repeat for the other end. This will form a contrasting strip on each edge of the back piece. See the photograph *opposite* for details. Narrowly hem any raw edges.

8 Fold the back slipcover in half crosswise, right sides facing. Sew along the short ends. Clip the corners and trim the seam allowances. Turn the cover to the right side and slip it over the chair back.

What You'll Need...

- ☐ basic picture frame with a wide border
- ☐ self-adhesive scrapbooking trims in a single theme

just beachy

❧ Take a plain wooden or plastic frame and add scrapbooking trims to create a customized frame that shows off a special memory.

1 Clean the frame and remove any labels, glass, or trims.

2 Arrange the trims to create a pleasing vignette. Remove the backings and stick the trims to the frame.

for your guys

only

Surprise the men on your list with handcrafted gifts made from some of their favorite things.

license for fun

❧ Rev up mornings with a mirror trimmed in old license plates. The ones used here are well-rusted for an understated look; newer ones would give a brighter, more graphic appearance.

1 Line up the license plates log-cabin style. See the photograph *opposite* for placement. Measure the outside dimensions and the size of the center opening. Have the mirror cut to the center opening size.

2 Cut the plywood ½ inch smaller all around than the outside dimensions so the license plate hanging holes will not be covered by the plywood base. Paint the plywood black; let dry. Draw diagonal lines from corner to corner, forming a large X.

3 Drill two holes for hanging at each upper corner. Place the holes 4 inches down from the top. Drill one hole 4 inches in from the outer edge and a second hole 5 inches in from the outer edge. Repeat for the other side. Thread the wire through one set of holes and twist it on itself to secure. Repeat with the other end of the wire and the other

set of holes to create a wire hanger on the back of the plywood base.

4 Place the mirror in the center of the plywood by aligning the corners with the X. Draw around the mirror, then set it aside.

5 Apply mirror mastic within the mirror lines and press the mirror into place. Apply mirror mastic to the remaining exposed plywood and put the license plates in place. Place heavy books or other items on the frame and let it dry for 24 to 48 hours.

tie one on

❧ Line up old neckties to create a simple patchwork pillow. What a great way to remember fashions, lifestyles, and careers of bygone days.

1 Measuring from the point up, cut the neckties to the desired length; this will be the height of the pillow. Remove the stitching

and labels from the ties and press them flat. Refold the ties so the edges are straight and press again. This will create the straight strips for the patchwork.

2 Position the ties on the canvas so all the points align and small triangles of canvas show between the points. Invisibly slip-stitch the ties to the canvas. Cut the canvas to size, allowing ½-inch seam allowances.

3 Cover the cord with the contrasting fabric. Baste the cord to the pillow front along the stitching line.

4 Cut the backing fabric to match the pillow front. With right sides facing, sew around the pillow, leaving an opening for turning and stuffing. Clip the corners and trim the seam allowances.

5 Turn the pillow to the right side. Stuff it very firmly with fiberfill and slip-stitch the opening closed.

What You'll Need...

- ☐ 6 or more old neckties
- ☐ 14×18-inch piece of natural canvas for the front and same size piece of fabric for the back
- ☐ sewing thread and hand-quilting needle
- ☐ cord for covering
- ☐ contrasting fabric for cord cover
- ☐ polyester fiberfill

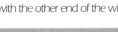
What You'll Need...

- ☐ 4 old or new same-size license plates
- ☐ mirror that will be cut to size
- ☐ ¼-inch-thick plywood scrap
- ☐ black paint
- ☐ drill and small bit
- ☐ wire for hanging
- ☐ mirror mastic adhesive and caulking gun
- ☐ books or other heavy items

138

What You'll Need...

- plastic wheel cover
- battery-operated clockwork and long clock hands (available at crafts stores)
- drill and drill bit
- black cardstock scraps
- industrial-strength glue

What You'll Need...

- wooden plane
- awl or hammer and nail
- drill with a 5/16-inch drill bit
- masking tape
- sandpaper

just plane fun

༄ Turn an old wood plane into an all-in-one desk set simply by drilling a few holes. Look for inexpensive or damaged planes at flea markets, garage sales, and auctions.

1 Mark spots for holes in the flat surface of the plane, spacing them evenly to form a grid pattern. The plane shown *above* is designed with four rows of three holes. Using an awl, make a hole at each point.

2 Determine the depth of the holes. Wrap tape around the bit at this point to help keep the holes at an equal depth. For example, if the holes are 1 inch deep, place the tape 1 inch from the end of the bit.

3 Drill a hole at each marked point, taking care to drill straight down and not at an angle. Drill only to

the edge of the tape. Lightly sand around each hole to remove shavings and burrs.

4 Place a small strip of tape in the bottom of the shavings hole to seal the opening beside the blade. Fill the shavings slot with paper clips and the holes with pencils and pens.

time for wheelies

༄ Reflect a love for cars with a wheel cover that is converted into a clock. Look for inexpensive but stylish plastic hubcaps at auto parts stores.

1 With a drill bit the same size as the clock movement post, drill a hole in the center of the wheel cover. Assemble the clockwork through the hole according to the clock package instructions.

2 Cut long rectangular strips for the clock hand covers. Glue them to the clock hands so the hands are more prominent. Attach the hands to the clockwork.

140

the forefront.

Let kids be kids and do what comes naturally—be creative. Clear off the table, spread out the supplies, and host a crafting party where kids make gifts for all the people they love.

JUST for KIDS

kids' crafting party

Turn a play date into a crafting party where imaginations rule.

Instead of having kids gather to watch movies or play video games, guide them to some holiday crafting. Plan one or more crafts projects, spread out the supplies, provide a little guidance, and let their natural creativity take over. Add a little hot chocolate and some cookies to the mix, and they're sure to have a great time—and take home gifts they'll be proud to give.

bottle cap baubles

Beads, buttons, and ball chain turn plain bottle caps into jewelry that's both funky and functional. Scrapbooking words and stickers embellish the matching earrings and bracelet on *page 144*. All the materials are from the crafts store.

Join the bottle caps to each other using jump rings. See the photographs *left* and on *page 143* for details. Use another jump ring to attach the bead strand.

5 Place a ball-chain loop connector to each end of the chain. Attach the connectors to the bottle caps with jump rings. Attach a small button to each loop connector with wire.

FOR THE BRACELET

1 Determine the length of the bracelet and lay out the bottle caps. Mark where they will connect and make holes as described *above*.

2 Using a circle template the same size as the bottle cap, cut out words or designs from decorative papers and sticker sheets. Several items can be combined collage-style or a single circle can be used. See the photograph *below* for design ideas.

3 Adhere the decorations to the bottle caps using the self-adhesive sticker backing or double-sided tape. Cover the bottle cap with three coats of paper sealer, letting the cap dry between each coat.

4 Join the bottle caps with jump rings. Attach the toggle clasp to the bracelet strand with jump rings.

See the photographs *above and on page 143*

What You'll Need...

- [ ] blank bottle caps (available at scrapbooking and crafts stores)
- [ ] awl and hammer
- [ ] sandpaper or metal file
- [ ] embellishments such as beads, buttons, decorative papers, sheet-style paper stickers, and grain-size gold crafting marbles
- [ ] industrial-strength glue
- [ ] jewelry findings: jump rings, head pins, ball chain, earring hooks, bracelet toggle clasp, and ball-chain loop connectors
- [ ] round-nose pliers
- [ ] wire cutters
- [ ] silver wire
- [ ] circle template (optional)
- [ ] small sharp scissors or crafts knife and cutting surface
- [ ] double-sided tape
- [ ] paper sealer (available in the paper or glue departments of crafts stores)
- [ ] epoxy stickers (available in scrapbooking stores and departments)
- [ ] gold glitter dimensional paint in a squeeze bottle

FOR THE EARRINGS

1 As described *far left*, make a hole in each bottle cap for attaching the earring wire.

2 Press an epoxy sticker to the center of each cap. Outline the stickers with dimensional paint.

3 Working over a bowl, shake the tiny gold marbles over the wet paint. Gently shake away the excess marbles. See the photograph *above left* for details. Let dry overnight.

4 Using jump rings, attach the earring

GENERAL INSTRUCTIONS

To connect the caps to each other or the jewelry findings, you will need to make holes in the rims. If necessary, mark the spot where the hole will be needed. Place the bottle cap on a wood block, brick, or other hard surface. Using an awl and hammer, make the necessary small holes in the rim. Sand or file from the back side to remove any sharp edges.

FOR THE NECKLACE

1 Lay out the placement of the bottle caps. See the photographs *above and on page 143* for details. Mark the points where the bottle caps will join and where the hanging chain will attach. Make holes as described *above*.

2 Using industrial-strength glue, adhere a larger button to the bottle cap. Glue a smaller button on top of the first button.

3 While the glue dries, thread beads onto a head pin. Bend the end of the head pin over to create a loop. Trim away any excess wire.

let's do lunch boxes

〰 Unadorned metal boxes provide the perfect canvas for decoupage designs—and the perfect container for games, dance supplies, and other items that need to be organized.

1 Determine the theme for the box and collect embellishments to carry out that theme. Cut out any words or designs from decorative papers. Arrange all the elements on the box lid, then set them to the side in the same pattern. For interest, layer several items on top of each other. See the photographs *below* for ideas.

2 Brush the back of the decorative papers with decoupage medium and use it as glue to adhere the papers to the box front. Continue adding papers and

decoupage medium until all the papers are in place and covered with three or more coats of decoupage medium. Let the box dry completely.

3 Add stickers and any other embellishments. Use double-sided tape for lightweight items and industrial-strength glue for heavier items. Let dry.

4 If desired, decorate the inside of the lid in the same manner and wrap the handle in ribbon or other trims.

paintbrush pals

❧ These kids are bright-eyed and bushy-haired. Start with a wide paintbrush as the base. Cover all but the bristles with polymer clay. Add clay faces and other details to turn the brushes into mirrors, hanging pegs, or funky room decorations.

1 Prepare the bristle hair. For the girl, wait until the brush is completely finished, then divide the bristles into three sections. Tie the sections with rubber bands and ribbons for pigtails. For the boy, trim approximately 1 inch from the bristles. Cut the edge with choppy diagonal motions. For the cat, remove a 1-inch-wide section from the center of the bristles so they are only about ½ inch long. Trim the remaining sections into points for ears.

2 Cover the work surface with freezer paper, placing the slick side up. Knead the clay for the face color with your hands, mixing colors if necessary. For the cat, mix several colors and knead only until the colors are marbleized. Mix enough of this clay to also cover the handle. Roll the clay to an even ¼-inch thickness.

What You'll Need...

- [ ] 4-inch-wide stain brush with natural bristles and unfinished handle
- [ ] freezer paper
- [ ] polymer clay (such as Premo! Sculpey) in the desired colors; white may be mixed with colors to achieve the desired shade
- [ ] sculpting tools for clay, including carving and rolling tools
- [ ] ruler
- [ ] oven thermometer
- [ ] baking tray lined with foil
- [ ] gel-style instant-stick glue (see page 158 for suggested glue)

FOR THE BOY:
- [ ] wooden cabinet knob with screw
- [ ] screwdriver

FOR THE GIRL:
- [ ] thin colored wire
- [ ] wire cutters
- [ ] beads
- [ ] mirror to fit the brush
- [ ] rope-style cording

4 To attach a hanging peg (such as for the boy brush), place the knob over the hole in the handle of the brush. Tighten the screw from the back until the knob is secure. Knead together the colors desired for the handle and roll the clay to an even 1/4-inch thickness. Cut and wrap the clay in the same manner as for the face.

7 Remove the wire from the girl's ears. String a new wire with beads for earrings and insert that wire into the holes in the ears, twisting it back onto itself. Style her hair as described in Step 1. See the photograph opposite for details. Using instant-stick glue, attach a mirror to the back if desired. Glue cording around the mirror.

147

5 Knead and roll out the clay for the face pieces, including ears for the boy and girl. Cut or sculpt all the face pieces and press them onto the face clay. See the photograph above for details. If desired, run a wire through the girl's ears to later attach earrings.

6 Using an oven thermometer, preheat the oven to 275 degrees. Place the finished brushes on a baking sheet lined with foil and bake as directed on the clay instructions. Let the brushes cool completely.

3 Using a ruler as a guide, cut the clay in a rectangle large enough to cover the entire top of the brush. Wrap the clay around the brush. See the photograph above. Press the clay to the brush and cut away any excess clay.

bookmark babes

Wooden skewers, pre-made polymer clay designs, beads, and wire are the makings for bookmarks that have as much personality as the kids who craft them.

FOR EACH BOOKMARK

1 Paint the skewer the desired colors. Let the paint dry completely.

2 Cut an 8-inch length of wire and the desired amount of material for the skirt. Wrap the skirt around the skewer and wind wire around the top edge to secure it to the skewer. Snip off the excess wire or shape it into coils using the pliers. Add a dot of glue to hold the skirt in place. NOTE: The skirt may be omitted for the millefiori bookmarks. Wrap the wire around the skewer, winding the ends into coils. See the photographs *below* for details. Glue the wire in place.

3 Add beads above the skirt to form the torso. Cut a 10-inch length of wire and fold it in half. Measure in 2 inches from each end of the wire and fold the ends back. Twist the ends to the wire to secure them. This will form two arm loops. NOTE: Omit the arms for the millefiori bookmarks.

4 Place the skewer into the original fold at the center of the wire. Wrap the wire around the skewer to form the rest of the torso. Add more beads for the neck.

5 Cut another 10-inch length of wire. Wrap one end around the tip of the skewer leaving a long tail of wire. Add a dot of glue over the coiled wire, then slip a bead over the wire and skewer tip.

6 Thread the wire tail through the polymer bead. Glue more wires into the bead if desired. Twist the wires together and slide a bead or beads over them. Using pliers, coil the wire ends. See the photographs *below* for details.

148

What You'll Need...

- [ ] clear vinyl tubing in $^3/_{16}$-, $^1/_8$-, $^1/_4$-, and $^3/_8$-inch diameters (available at hardware stores)
- [ ] sharp scissors
- [ ] scraps of decorative papers
- [ ] wooden skewer
- [ ] wire
- [ ] wire cutters
- [ ] round- and long-nose pliers
- [ ] assorted beads and charms
- [ ] jump rings
- [ ] key rings and lanyard hooks

get with the bead

❧ Key chains are hot, whether they hold keys or not. These fobs hook onto backpacks, zipper pulls, and instrument cases, too. Colorful papers coiled inside clear tubing mix it up with regular beads for one-of-a-kind snap-on trims.

1 Cut the tubing into short pieces ranging from $^1/_2$ to 1 inch long.

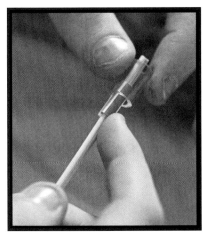

2 To make the paper-filled beads, cut a long strip of decorative paper the same width as the length of the tube. Tightly roll the paper around the skewer with the decorative side out. Slip the skewer and paper partially into the tube. See the photograph *above* for details. Slide the skewer out of the paper coil and gently push the paper the rest of the way into the tube. The paper will unwind and fill the tube. Slide a wire through the center of the paper and tube. Add a bead the same or larger diameter as the tube to each end. Loop the wire ends and snip away any excess wire. This will keep the paper in the tube and provide loops for stringing.

3 To make bead-filled tubes, cut a wire longer than the tube. Make a loop at one end. Slide on a bead that is the same or larger diameter than the tube. Add enough small beads to fill the tube. Slip the tube over the beads. Add another larger bead and end with another loop. Trim away the excess wire.

4 To assemble the fobs, make as many paper-filled and bead-filled tubes as desired. Line them up to create the design you want. Join the loops with jump rings. Purchased beads may be added.

5 For the end bead, leave the wire long and coil it. See the photographs *above right* and *right* for details. If desired, add a charm to the end. Attach the first bead to a key ring or lanyard using jump rings.

149

pet couture

You dress for success. Why shouldn't your four-legged friends?

Whether they're one-of-a-kind cats from the local shelter or pooches with a pedigree a mile long, today's pets are pampered. Designer-style jewelry, clothing, beds, and blankets are just a few of the items every pet seems to be needing.

What You'll Need...

- [ ] necktie from the men's or boy's clothing department
- [ ] fabric glue
- [ ] thick elastic cord
- [ ] pony beads to match the tie

all business

🌫 Mr. Bentley is ready for a serious day of play in his striped necktie. Make the tie whatever size fits your pet simply by cutting a man's or boy's necktie.

NOTE: When making pet jewelry, do not use beading wire. For safety, use stringing material that will stretch or break if the pet catches the jewelry on something. Use small beads to prevent choking.

1 Tie the necktie in your favorite way, adjusting it to be the proper length for the dog or cat. Cut away the excess length, leaving the underneath piece about 1 inch shorter than the tie. Glue the narrow under piece to the back of the tie. Run a bead of glue along the cut edge to prevent fraying. Let the glue dry.

2 Cut elastic cording to fit the dog's or cat's neck, adding 1½ inches for tying and comfort. Thread the pony beads onto the elastic, leaving enough elastic for tying.

3 Loosen the upper portion of the tie's knot with your finger. Run the beaded elastic through the knot. Tighten the necktie knot over the beads. Add more beads if needed. Tie the elastic into a tight square knot. Slip the knot under one of the beads to conceal it.

pure pleasure

〜 Ms. Brooke isn't shy when it comes to dressing up. Her double-strand necklace is made from glass beads and coordinates with her favorite coat—the one she wears everywhere.

1 Measure the dog's or cat's neck, allowing for the necklace to drape slightly. Lay the beads out to the desired lengths and patterns. Place the pendant bead at the center of the longer strand.

2 Cut the beading cords several inches longer than the bead strands and string the beads onto the cords.

3 Tightly tie the ends of the cords to the first and third loops of the closure pieces. (Using a triple-strand closure spaces the two beaded strands farther apart than using a double-strand closure. The center loop can be snipped off if desired.) Run the ends of the cord back into the beads.

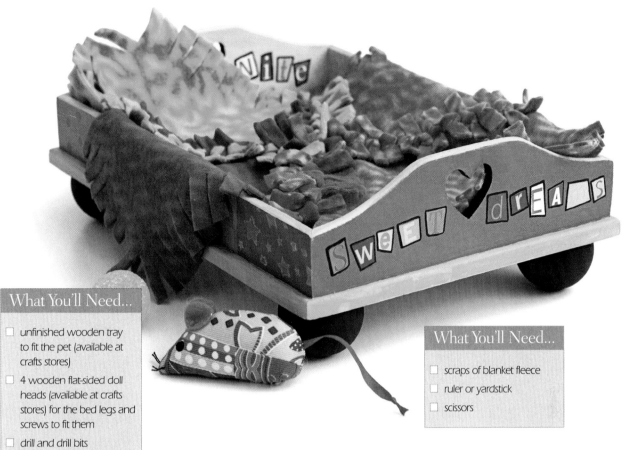

153

What You'll Need...

- [ ] unfinished wooden tray to fit the pet (available at crafts stores)
- [ ] 4 wooden flat-sided doll heads (available at crafts stores) for the bed legs and screws to fit them
- [ ] drill and drill bits
- [ ] sandpaper and tack cloth
- [ ] assorted acrylic paints
- [ ] disposable foam paintbrushes
- [ ] letter stickers
- [ ] decoupage medium

What You'll Need...

- [ ] scraps of blanket fleece
- [ ] ruler or yardstick
- [ ] scissors

feline furniture

Most cats love to curl up in small spaces. Give your kitty a custom-made bed fashioned from a purchased wooden tray so it can snooze in style.

1. Fit the doll heads to the bottom of the tray for legs. Drill holes to attach the doll heads to the tray but do not attach them yet. Sand the tray and doll heads and wipe with a tack cloth.

2. Paint the tray and doll heads as desired. Paint a second coat if needed, sanding between coats. Add patterns if desired.

3. Adhere letter stickers to the head, foot, and sides of the bed to spell out your favorite pet phrases or names. Paint the lettered surfaces with three or more coats of decoupage medium, allowing the medium to dry between coats.

4. Attach the doll-head legs to the tray bottom with screws.

knots of appeal

Almost every pet loves to make a nest for napping. Make a fleece blanket to any size that fits your pet or its bed. The knots and fringe turn the cuddly blanket into a toy when play takes precedence over sleep.

1. Determine the final size of the blanket. Divide this measurement into four equal quadrants by dividing both the length and the width in half. For example, if the desired finished size is 10×12 inches, each quadrant would be 5×6 inches. Add four inches to each side. This would bring the 5×6-inch quadrants to 13×14 inches.

2. Cut four pieces of fleece to the size determined. Mark a 4-inch square in each corner of each piece; cut away that square.

3. Cut all the sides into 4-inch-long pieces of fringe with each piece of fringe measuring ½ inch wide.

4. Lay out the pieces in the pattern in which they fit together. Tie two pairs of blocks together using the fringe. Tie the two strips together. See the photograph *below* for details. Do not tie the knots too tightly. Trim the knotted fringe if desired.

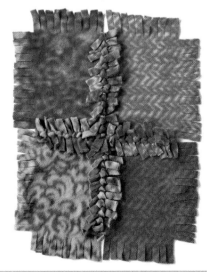

project details

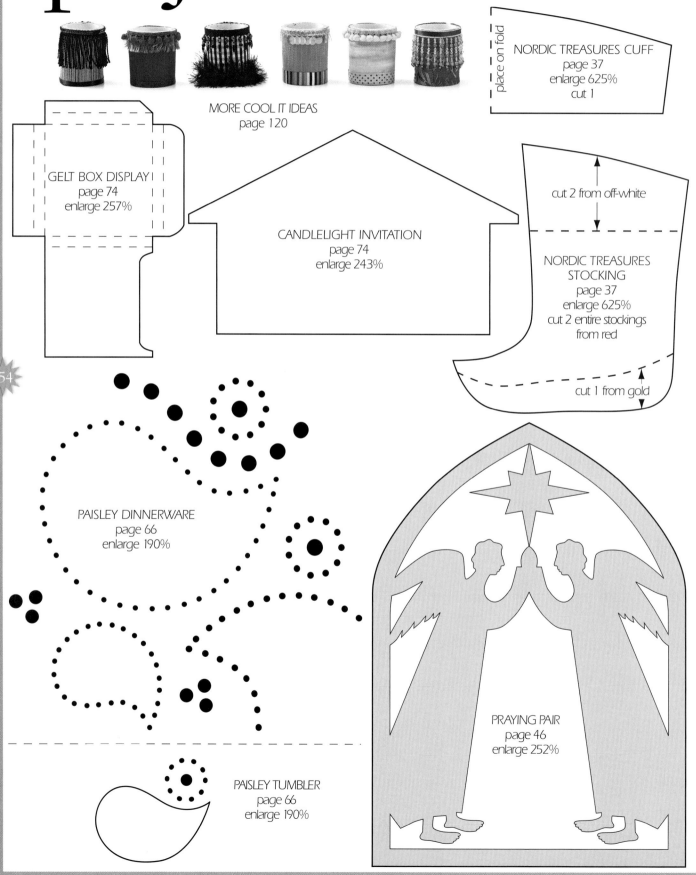

MORE COOL IT IDEAS
page 120

NORDIC TREASURES CUFF
page 37
enlarge 625%
cut 1

place on fold

GELT BOX DISPLAY
page 74
enlarge 257%

CANDLELIGHT INVITATION
page 74
enlarge 243%

cut 2 from off-white

NORDIC TREASURES
STOCKING
page 37
enlarge 625%
cut 2 entire stockings
from red

cut 1 from gold

154

PAISLEY DINNERWARE
page 66
enlarge 190%

PRAYING PAIR
page 46
enlarge 252%

PAISLEY TUMBLER
page 66
enlarge 190%

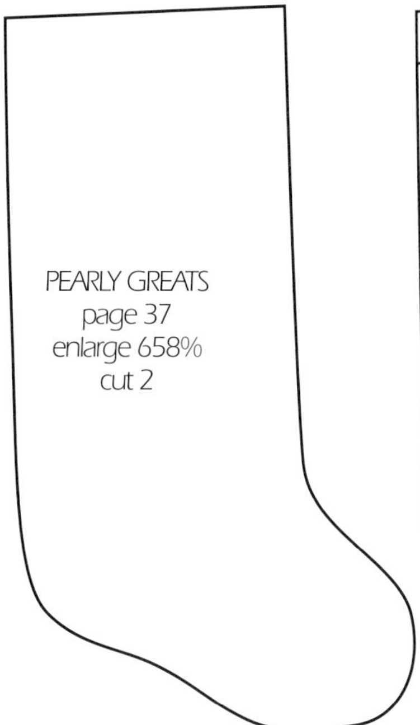

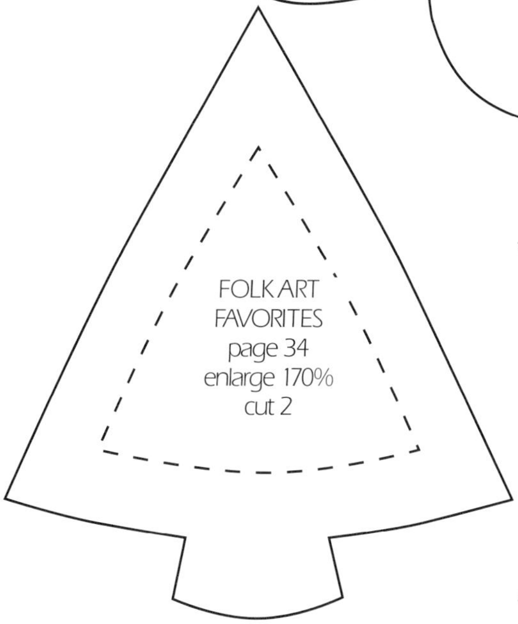

PEARLY GREATS
page 37
enlarge 658%
cut 2

FOLD

LUCKY
PENNIES
page 37
enlarge 653%
cut 2

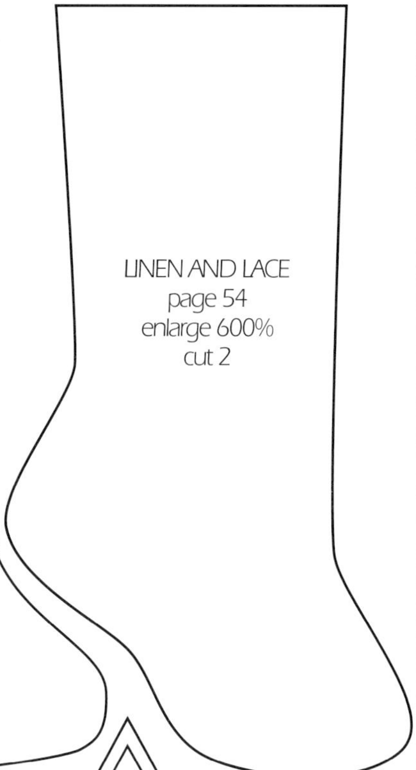

LINEN AND LACE
page 54
enlarge 600%
cut 2

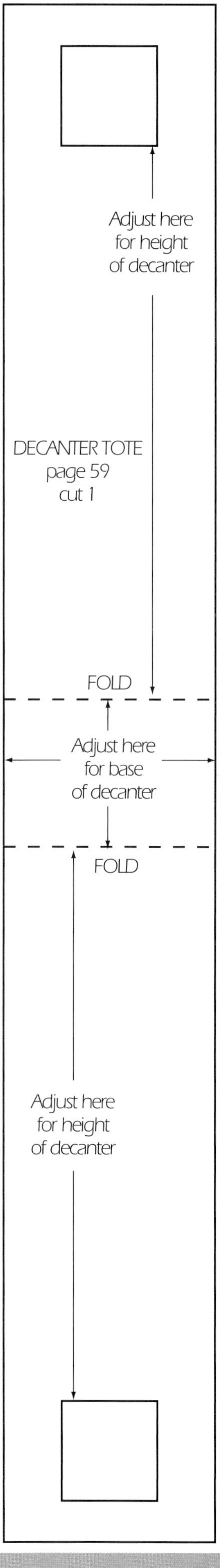

Adjust here
for height
of decanter

DECANTER TOTE
page 59
cut 1

FOLD

Adjust here
for base
of decanter

155

FOLD

FOLK ART
FAVORITES
page 34
enlarge 170%
cut 2

FRIENDLY SHAKE
page 75
enlarge 334%

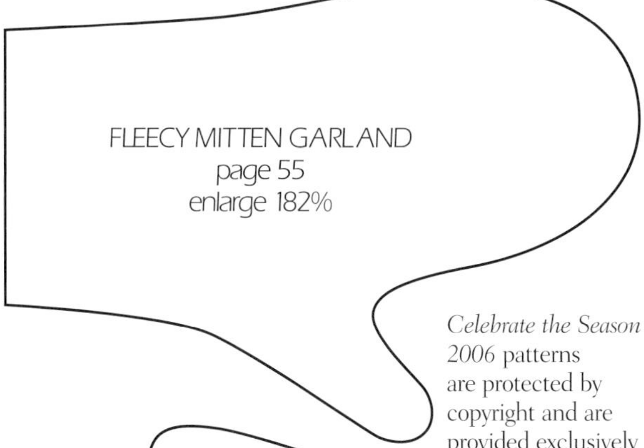

Adjust here
for height
of decanter

FLEECY MITTEN GARLAND
page 55
enlarge 182%

*Celebrate the Season
2006* patterns
are protected by
copyright and are
provided exclusively
for our readers.
Purchasers of this
book have permission
to make a photocopy
of these patterns to
make the projects
in the book for their
personal use.

FIESTA STAR AND QUAD
pages 78–87
for apron enlarge 245%,
for recipe cards
use at 34%

GIFT BAG MITTENS
page 61
shown at 100%
cut 4

project details *continued*

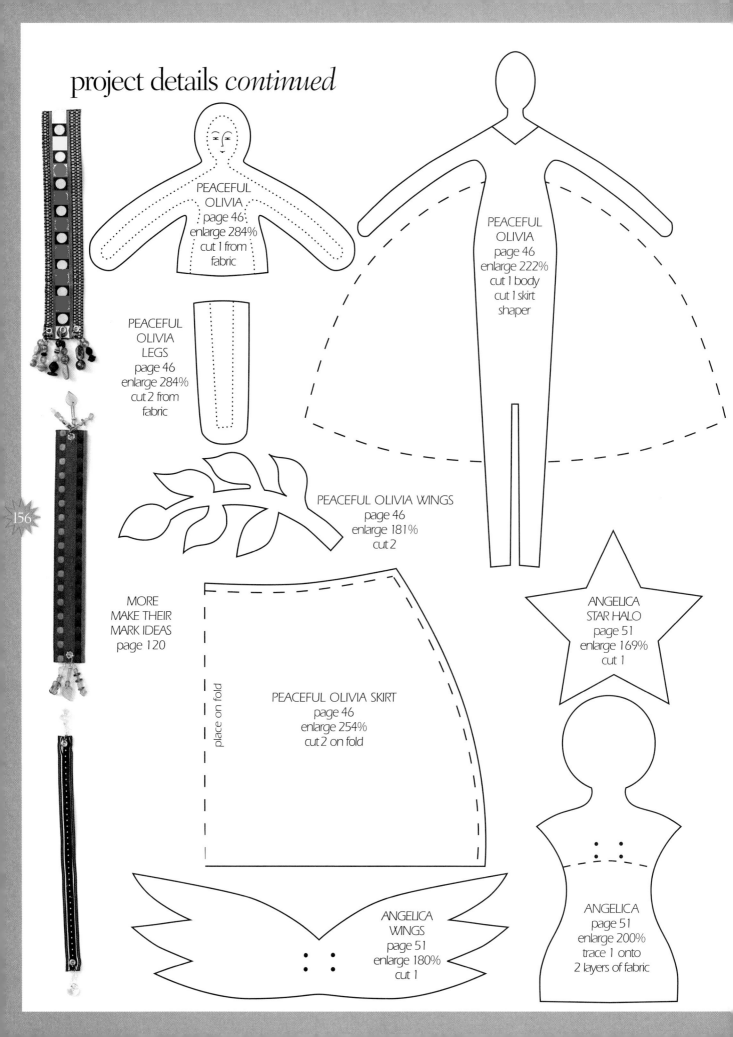

PEACEFUL
OLIVIA
page 46
enlarge 284%
cut 1 from
fabric

PEACEFUL
OLIVIA
page 46
enlarge 222%
cut 1 body
cut 1 skirt
shaper

PEACEFUL
OLIVIA
LEGS
page 46
enlarge 284%
cut 2 from
fabric

PEACEFUL OLIVIA WINGS
page 46
enlarge 181%
cut 2

156

MORE
MAKE THEIR
MARK IDEAS
page 120

place on fold

PEACEFUL OLIVIA SKIRT
page 46
enlarge 254%
cut 2 on fold

ANGELICA
STAR HALO
page 51
enlarge 169%
cut 1

ANGELICA
WINGS
page 51
enlarge 180%
cut 1

ANGELICA
page 51
enlarge 200%
trace 1 onto
2 layers of fabric

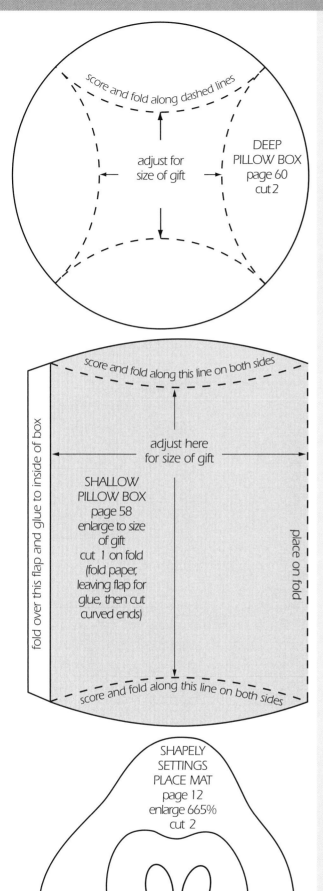

score and fold along dashed lines

adjust for
size of gift

DEEP
PILLOW BOX
page 60
cut 2

score and fold along this line on both sides

fold over this flap and glue to inside of box

adjust here
for size of gift

SHALLOW
PILLOW BOX
page 58
enlarge to size
of gift
cut 1 on fold
(fold paper,
leaving flap for
glue, then cut
curved ends)

place on fold

score and fold along this line on both sides

SHAPELY
SETTINGS
PLACE MAT
page 12
enlarge 665%
cut 2

PROJECT SKILL LEVEL

157

credits & sources

Unless otherwise stated, photo styling by Marisa Dirks and Jilann Severson. Food styling by Charles Worthington. Photographs by Jay Wilde.

cover, page 4: wreath design, Jim Williams; photograph, Peter Krumhardt; crystal snowflake ornaments, Swarovski Christmas Ornament 1999, 2001, and 2005, Swarovski North America Ltd., 800/426-3088, www.swarovski.com
page 6: photograph, Peter Krumhardt
pages 8–13: designs, Jim Williams
pages 14–17: designs, Sue Banker
pages 28–33: designs, Joann Brantley
pages 34–37: designs, Suzi Carson
pages 46–51: designs, Suzi Carson; photograph page 51, Peter Krumhardt; Holo*Gram Silver and Holo*Gram Gold glitter by Glitterex Corporation, 908/272-9121, www.glitterex.com
pages 58–61: designs, Marisa Dirks
pages 62–63: Study in Contrast, Starry, Starry Sight, and Lights Fantastic designs, Jilann Severson; Music to the Eyes design, Sue Banker; Bowl of Baubles design, Gayle Schadendorf
page 65: photograph, Peter Krumhardt
pages 66–71: designs, Sue Banker; Liquitex Glossies glass paint available at crafts stores nationwide

pages 76–77: Polka-Dot Parade, In Stitches, and Santa's Bags designs, Sue Banker; Visions of Sugarplums design, Joann Brantley
pages 78–87: Crunchy Corn Snack Mix, Avocado and Apple Salad, Cornmeal Pecan Biscuits, and Pork, Poblano, and Sweet Potato Stew recipes developed by Shelli McConnell; project and decorating designs, Gayle Schadendorf; Delta PermEnamel glass paint available at crafts stores nationwide; Mediterranean Swirl Bowls from Better Homes and Gardens™ Collection exclusively by Home Interiors & Gifts; 888/377-5297, www.homeinteriors.com
pages 96–101: Crab and Horseradish Havarti Dip and Frosty Raspberry Margaritas recipes developed by Shelli McConnell
pages 102–111: Spinach Salad with Leeks and Pancetta, Roasted Lamb with Olive Tapenade, Root Vegetable Mash, Mushroom Medley, Thyme-Roasted Beets, and Prosciutto-and-Basil-Stuffed Turkey Breast recipes developed by Shelli McConnell; project and decorating designs, Gayle Schadendorf
page 112: photograph, Peter Krumhardt
pages 114–123: Gingered Cranberry-Orange Balls and Peppermint Stars recipes developed by Shelli McConnell; Cool It, Make Their Mark, and Nap of Luxury designs, Jilann Severson; Beads of Light, Bathing Beauty Scented Bath Salts decanters, and Tea Time designs, Marisa Dirks; Bathing Beauty Scented Bath Salts design/recipe, Karen Weir-Jimerson

pages 124–129: designs, Gayle Schadendorf
pages 130–135: designs, Sharon Widdop
pages 136–139: designs, Jim Williams
page 140: photograph, Peter Krumhardt
pages 144–151: designs, Kristin Detrick; lunch boxes available from Tin Town, 310/921-9653, www.tintown. com; Quick Grip industrial-strength glue from Beacon Adhesives available at crafts stores nationwide, 914/699-3400, www. beaconcreates.com; Premo! Sculpey polymer clay from Polyform Products available at crafts stores nationwide, 847/427-0020, www.sculpey.com; gel-style instant-stick Instant Krazy Glue Gel available at crafts stores nationwide; polymer face beads (#161770PB) and millefiori beads (search under fimo) available from Fire Mountain Gems, 800/423-2319, www.firemountaingems. com
pages 152–154: designs, Jilann Severson; dogs, Jordan Standard Schnauzers, 651/686-5305
page 155: designs, Kristin Detrick